MORE
THAN A
BUILDING

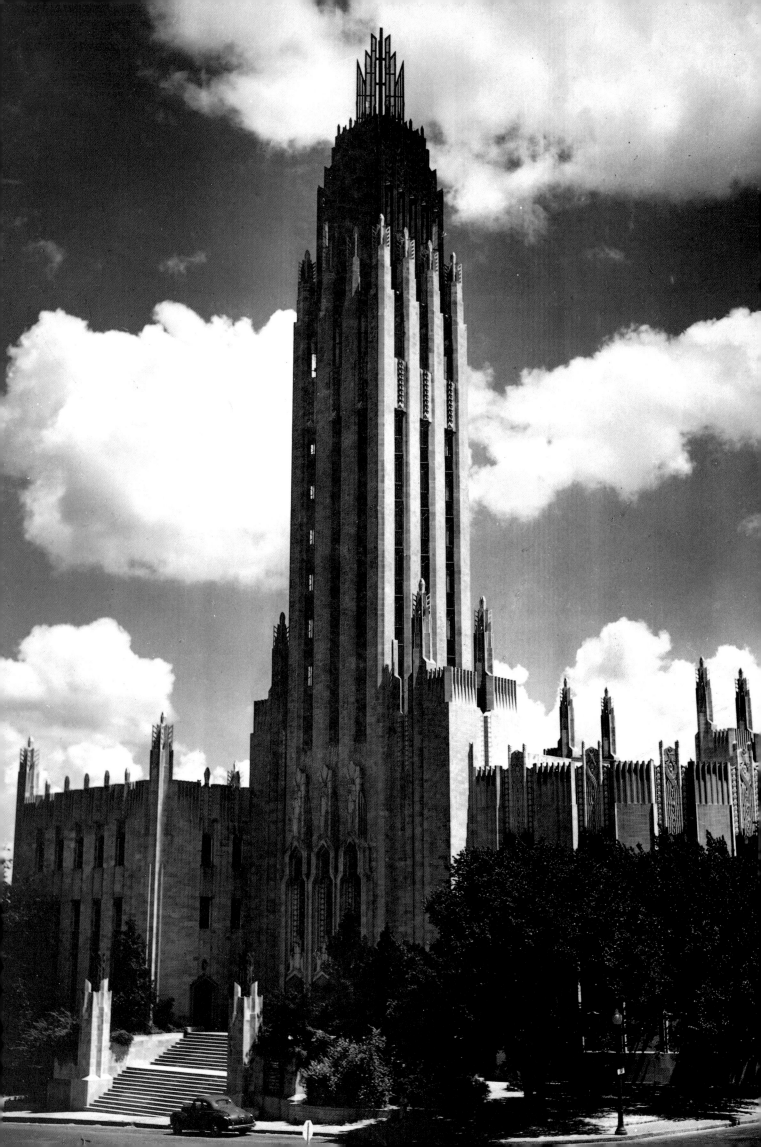

MORE THAN A BUILDING

THE FIRST CENTURY

OF BOSTON AVENUE

UNITED METHODIST

CHURCH

JO BETH HARRIS

THE CENTENNIAL
CELEBRATION COMMITTEE
BOSTON AVENUE UNITED
METHODIST CHURCH
1 9 9 3
<<<<<<
TULSA

COUNCIL OAK PUBLISHING CO., INC.
1350 EAST FIFTEENTH STREET
TULSA, OKLAHOMA 74120

SYMBOLISM CAPTIONS BY SHEILA PARR

DESIGNED BY CAROL HARALSON
COLOR PLATE PHOTOGRAPHY BY
DAVID HALPERN (PAGES 17, 18, 19, 20, 21, 22,
23, 24, 25, 26 BOTTOM, 28, 29, 30,
31 BOTTOM, 32, AND COVER);
JOHNNY GONZALEZ (PAGES 26 TOP AND 27);
AND HAROLD REYNOLDS (PAGE 31 TOP)

PRINTED IN HONG KONG THROUGH PALACE PRESS

*To the twenty-one pastors who have
guided this congregation during its first
century, including Mouzon Biggs,
pastor at the church's centennial, who
exemplifies the best of all those who
have gone before.*

MORE THAN A BUILDING

CONTENTS

A C K N O W L E D G E M E N T S

Records and photos in the church archives provided much of what we know of the church's history, and my heartfelt thanks goes to the members of the History and Archives Committee, past and present, for their patient gathering and preservation of those records. Whenever possible, original records and letters were used as resource materials. Archivists Martha Jo and John Bradley were a source of constant help and support, and without them, the book could never have been completed in the allotted time.

My thanks to Mary and Doc Metzel who provided so much valuable information and encouragement; to Sheila Parr for her help and knowledge of the church building and its symbolism; to Jim Dixon for the generous loan of his wonderful collection of Tulsa books which provided so much Tulsa history; and to Dr. Biggs, the church staff, and members of the congregation who were unfailingly helpful and cooperative.

I feel particularly close to those whom I interviewed for the "Memories" segments, and am very grateful for the facts, treasured photographs, and especially for the memories which they shared with me and the readers of this book. Most of all, my thanks to Sally Dennison for her skillful editing and for helping play "sleuth" when information was contradictory or details were elusive. We shared the goal of making the book as accurate and as complete as possible in recording all that went into making this church one of Tulsa's greatest treasures.

Writing this book has been a joy, and I am grateful to the Centennial Committee which selected me as its author. I am honored to have been given the opportunity to help chronicle the first one hundred years of Boston Avenue Church.

Jo Beth Harris

MORE THAN A BUILDING

THE FIRST CENTURY
OF BOSTON AVENUE UNITED METHODIST CHURCH

INTRODUCTION

The Boston Avenue United Methodist Church stands today in the heart of downtown Tulsa, Oklahoma, fulfilling its designer's purpose "to assure the hurried passerby of the reality of the Infinite." The beauty and remarkable design of the building make it one of the major features of the city, and it draws visitors from all over the world.

But the building at Thirteenth and Boston is only the home of the real church. The real church is a congregation of men and women who have worked hard through the past one hundred years to build and maintain Boston Avenue's programs, facilities, ministries, and missions. As they built the church, they were also building Tulsa. The story of Boston Avenue Church is the story of these people and of their vision, strength, faith, and dedication.

The church now known as "Boston Avenue" began as the Methodist Episcopal Church South. Tulsa was a village in Indian Territory, a settlement of whites who had come to trade with the Indians. It was a place of little wooden houses and mud streets with a population of about five hundred when the church was established in 1893.

Beginning with just seven people who met once a month in another church's rooms and in each other's homes, the future Boston Avenue Church quickly became a congregation of builders. Its pioneers first constructed their own rough brush arbor, then a wooden "box church," a modest brick church, an imposing pillared building, and then a magnificent cathedral which has become world famous.

Those Boston Avenue builders formed the cornerstone, not only of the church, but of the community. They soon built homes, hotels, hospitals, and businesses; constructed Tulsa's water systems and paved its streets. Members of the church were instrumental in Tulsa's first big oil strike and in establishing Tulsa as a city. Through the years they served as mayors and city officials, business and civic leaders. They helped make Tulsa the "Oil Capital," and they founded and operated many of the arts organizations and charities which have made it one of the nation's most liveable cities.

They built ambitiously during the boom times and tenaciously rode out the hard times, in a city where fortunes were amassed and lost, and often amassed again in a few short years. Theirs was a boundless optimism. In the Roaring Twenties they overspent the budget to build the beautiful "modern cathedral" at Thirteenth and Boston. Then, when the Depression came and they almost lost the building into which they had put so much time, money, love, and effort, they made the sacrifices necessary to save it. Through all the years, they never lost sight of the church's importance in their lives and the life of their city.

During the first century of this church's existence, twenty-one dedicated pastors each brought his own strengths and ideas, and each pastor's wife served the church and the community in her own way. From the beginning, women have played key roles in both the church and the community. Many earned places of prominence in the church and in civic affairs, but a far greater number worked just as hard, quietly and behind the scenes.

The men and women of Boston Avenue Church have married in the church, baptized their children here and reared them in its Sunday schools, and had their funerals preached by its ministers. Each Sunday they have met to seek God's guidance for themselves, for their church, and for their community.

The one hundredth birthday celebration of Boston Avenue Church is a celebration of this congregation of builders, a celebration of the spirit, strength, and dedication of those who have built the church, and the city in which it stands.

PORTRAIT
OF A
BUILDING

BOSTON AVENUE IN THE 1990s

SHOWN HERE SURROUNDED BY TULSA'S EXPRESSWAYS, BOSTON AVENUE CHURCH IS MORE THAN A WORK OF ART AND IT IS MORE THAN "JUST A BUILDING." IT IS A CREATION CONCEIVED AND DESIGNED "TO REMIND THE HURRIED PASSERBY OF THE REALITY OF THE INFINITE" AND "TO SERVE AS AN INSPIRATION FOR THE AGES."

WHEN DESIGNER ADAH ROBINSON LAUNCHED A SERIES OF LECTURES ABOUT THE CHURCH, SHE INSTRUCTED, "EVERY LINE EXPRESSES A THOUGHT. LOOK FOR IT."

MORE
THAN A
BUILDING

EXTERIOR

LIKE A SERMON IN STONE, THE CHURCH WAS INTENTIONALLY DESIGNED TO HONOR GOD AND TO
IDENTIFY ITS MEMBERS AS GOD'S PEOPLE. THE EXTERIOR IS ONE OF THE MOST SIGNIFICANT EXAMPLES
OF VERTICAL ART DECO ARCHITECTURE IN THE WORLD. THIS BOLD SCULPTURAL FORM WAS
SELECTED TO ACKNOWLEDGE THAT THE HUMAN MIND EVER REACHES TOWARD INFINITY.

Terra Cotta

God's light is portrayed in the golden color of the terra cotta used on the church's facade. The curved lines flowing downward symbolize the outpouring of God's love. This design is echoed in the sanctuary windows, domed ceiling, and altar mosaic. The seven pointed stars are reminders of the seven virtues: patience, purity, knowledge, long-suffering, kindness, love, and truth.

Praying Hands

One of the most popular and familiar features of the church, the sixty-two praying hands characterize it as a house of prayer. When interpreting her design of the praying hands, Adah Robinson noted, "Closed lines and horizontal lines have been associated with finality. Modern lines are flowing, upward, open, free. These modern hands, open, are confident of the receptivity of divine grace."

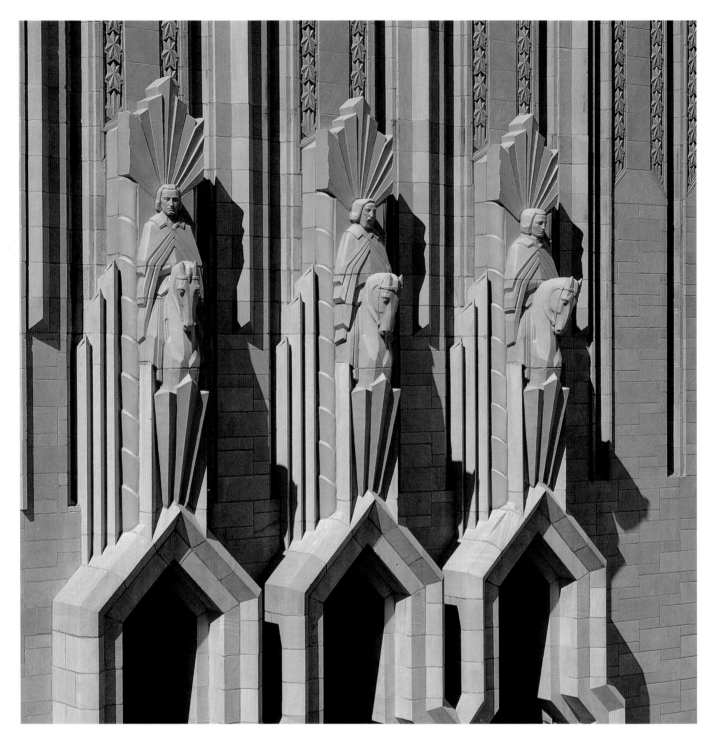

PORTRAIT SCULPTURES — CIRCUIT RIDERS

PORTRAIT SCULPTURES OVER THE TOWER ENTRANCES IDENTIFY THE MEMBERS AS METHODISTS AND
SERVE AS REMINDERS OF THE METHODIST HERITAGE. OVER THE SOUTH ENTRANCE IS A TRIBUTE IN
SCULPTURE TO THE CIRCUIT RIDERS WHO SPREAD METHODISM THROUGHOUT THE NEW COUNTRY.
ON THE RIGHT IS FRANCIS ASBURY, FATHER OF AMERICAN METHODISM. ON THE LEFT IS WILLIAM
MCKENDRIE, THE FIRST AMERICAN-BORN BISHOP. IN THE CENTER IS THE UNKNOWN CIRCUIT RIDER, A
COMPOSITE TO RECOGNIZE THOSE WHO SERVED IN INDIAN TERRITORY AND THIS AREA.

Portrait Sculptures — The Wesleys

The central figure at the north entrance is John Wesley, the founder of Methodism. To his right is his mother, Susanna, "his greatest educational, moral, and spiritual guide." The third figure is his brother Charles, the great writer of more than six thousand hymns.

ANGLED ARCHES

DISTINCTIVE ANGLED ARCHES "SUGGEST THE BLESSINGS OF GOD ON ALL WHO PASS
BENEATH." THIS ARCHED FORM IS USED THROUGHOUT THE CHURCH FOR DOORS,
WINDOWS, ETCHED GLASS, AND THE DETAILING OF THE BRASS HARDWARE.

OVERLEAF

THE SANCTUARY IN THE 1990S

SYMBOLS AND MOTIFS UNIFY OLD AND NEW IN THE SANCTUARY AS THEY APPEAR IN STAINED GLASS, PLASTER, OAK, BRASS, MOSAIC, AND IN THE OVERALL DESIGN. FOUR MASSIVE DOORS AND MULTIPLE AISLES SPEAK OF THE ACCESSIBILITY OF GOD. ALL LINES LEAD TO THE PULPIT AND FOCUS ON THE MESSAGE. THE TRITOMA MOTIF IS USED IN BANDS ON THE CHOIR STALLS AND PULPIT. ON THE MAJESTIC DOME OF THE CEILING IS A CIRCLE, ANCIENT SYMBOL OF THE INFINITE. GOD'S LIGHT AND GRACE ARE VISIBLE IN THE GOLDEN COLOR, FLOWING LINES, AND POINTED ARCHES. IN THE CENTER OF THE STAINED GLASS IS ANOTHER VARIATION ON THE COREOPSIS FLOWER.

COREOPSIS

THIS HARDY WILDFLOWER WHICH COVERS THE OKLAHOMA PRAIRIES IN EARLY SUMMER IS USED THROUGHOUT THE BUILDING TO SYMBOLIZE THE STRENGTH AND JOY OF A CHURCH ROOTED IN THE CHRISTIAN FAITH. HERE THE FLOWER CAN BE SEEN IN THE STAINED GLASS ON THE EXTERIOR DOORS AND IN THE SHAPE OF THE LIGHT FIXTURE OVERHANGING THE NORTH ENTRY HALL.

BEHIND THE PULPIT

THE PULPIT AREA APPOINTMENTS ARE SIMPLE BUT PRAYERFUL
IN EFFECT. THE MOTIFS USED ARE THE CIRCLE, LIGHT, AND
THE TRITOMA. THE MOSAIC, ADDED IN THE 1960S, CENTERS
ON THE CROSS WHICH BEARS THE IMPRESSION OF THE
RESURRECTED CHRIST.

THE ROSE CHAPEL

THE ROOM'S SIMPLICITY OF DESIGN CONVEYS PEACE AND
SPIRITUAL REPOSE.

BISHOPS HALL—VIEWED FROM THE SECOND FLOOR

WHEN THE EDUCATION WING WAS ADDED IN THE 1960S, THE FORMER PORTE COCHERE
BECAME AN ENTRY HALL FILLED WITH LIGHT, A SETTING FOR JOYFUL GATHERINGS, ESPECIALLY
DURING THE ADVENT SEASON.

BISHOPS HALL—VIEWED FROM THE NORTHWEST

DOORWAYS FROM BISHOPS HALL LEAD OUT TO AN ENCLOSED GARDEN. WALKWAYS CONNECT
THE ORIGINAL BUILDING TO THE EDUCATION WING, AND STAIRS LEAD DOWN TO THE COVERED
DRIVEWAY BENEATH THE NEWER BUILDING.

SOCIAL LOBBY

CONSIDERED AN UNUSUAL FEATURE IN A MODERN CHURCH, THE MAGNIFICENT GREAT HALL OF
THE SOCIAL LOBBY EMPHASIZES THE SPIRITUAL ATTITUDE TOWARD FELLOWSHIP. THE SOARING
HEIGHT OF THE CEILING SUGGESTS THE INFINITE POSSIBILITIES OF HUMAN KINDNESS AND
FELLOWSHIP. THE POWERFUL POINTED ARCH DESIGN IS A REMINDER OF GOD'S BLESSING ON ALL
WHO ENTER. THE SYMBOL FOR LIGHT IS MANIFESTED IN THE OPEN SPACE, THE STAINED GLASS
SKYLIGHTS, AND THE ATMOSPHERIC COLOR. MOSAICS WERE ORIGINALLY PLANNED FOR THE
RECESSED PANELS IN THE NORTH AND SOUTH ENDS OF THE GREAT HALL.

WALL LANTERNS

THE LAMPS WHICH LIGHT THE GREAT HALL CONTINUE MANY OF THE MOTIFS OF THE BUILDING,
INCLUDING THE TRITOMA. ANGLED ARCHES, ANGLED GLASS, AND THE FLOWING LINE ARE
EMBLEMATIC OF GOD'S GRACE.

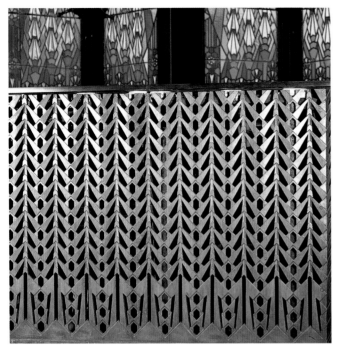

WOOD AND GLASS

THE RADIATOR SCREENS IN THE SANCTUARY AND THE STAINED-GLASS
WINDOWS ABOVE CARRY OUT THE TRITOMA THEME.

ROSE CHAPEL WINDOWS

THE WINDOWS IN THE ROSE CHAPEL, RICH IN COLOR AND DELICATE IN
DESIGN, JUSTIFY THE NAME OF THIS SPECIAL PLACE.

TRITOMA IN TERRAZZO

THE TRITOMA MOTIF FINDS EXPRESSION IN THE MARBLE FLOORS OF THE
ENTRY HALLS.

ROSE CHAPEL FRIEZE

PROCESSIONAL FIGURES ALTERNATING WITH TRITOMA ON THE FRIEZE ABOVE
THE ROSE CHAPEL WINDOWS EXPRESS DEVOTION.

TRITOMA

THIS OKLAHOMA WILDFLOWER, WITH ITS CASCADE OF BLOSSOMS DESCENDING FROM A STURDY STALK, SUGGESTS ORGANIZATION AND THE GENEROSITY OF THE FAITH. THE TRITOMA MOTIF, IN STYLIZED FORM, IS USED FREQUENTLY THROUGHOUT THE CHURCH.

TOWER CHAPEL

FINISHED IN THE 1960S, THE TOWER CHAPEL FEATURES A CANOPY OF ANGLED SURFACES WHICH RADIATE DOWNWARD FROM A CENTER BEAM.

OVERLEAF
SANCTUARY WINDOWS

THE DESIGN FOR THE SANCTUARY WINDOWS CALLED FOR "A NEW SET OF SYMBOLS TO EXPRESS THE VITALITY OF THE CHRISTIAN FAITH IN MID-AMERICA." THE MOST IMPORTANT OF THESE SYMBOLS IS LIGHT. TRANSPARENT BEVELED GLASS, VIBRANT COLORS, GOLDEN FLOWING LINES, AND TRIANGULAR CONSTRUCTION ADMIT MAXIMUM SUNLIGHT. TWO OTHER NEW SYMBOLS, THE COREOPSIS AND TRITOMA, APPEAR TOGETHER HERE.

MORE
THAN A
BUILDING

A GALLERY
OF
PASTORS

THE REVEREND E.B. CHENOWETH
1893-1896

THE REVEREND J.M. PORTER
1898-1899,1900

THE REVEREND A.M. BRANNON
1903-1905

THE REVEREND J.H. BALL
1906-1908

THE REVEREND ALFRED F. SMITH
1908-1910

THE REVEREND J.E. CARPENTER
1910

THE REVEREND PERCY KNICKERBOCKER
1910-1914

DR. LOUIS BARTON
1914-1918,
1919-1922

DR. JOHN RICE
1922-1927

DR. CLAUDE M. REVES
1927-1931

DR. CHARLES C. GRIMES
1931-1934

THE REVEREND FORNEY HUTCHINSON
1934-1939

DR. H. BASCOM WATTS
1939-1950

DR. PAUL V. GALLOWAY
1950-1960

DR. FINIS A. CRUTCHFIELD
1960-1972

DR. J. CHESS LOVERN
1972-1976

DR. JOHN RUSSELL
1976-1980

DR. M. MOUZON BIGGS
1980-

THE STRUGGLE TO BEGIN
THE REVEREND E. B. CHENOWETH - 1893-1896

In 1893, I was serving Cortez, Colorado, and Delores, Utah, when requests were being made for preachers to go to Oklahoma as it opened for settlement. With wife and baby, I volunteered to go. I attended the Indian Mission Conference at Vinita. I was sent to Tulsa, which was but a staked-out townsite. We reached there ten days before the opening and camped down on the bank of the river at the crossing. . . . Then I got busy. After obtaining consent of the railroad and section foreman, I cleared the brush across the new tracks and in front of the railroad right of way, all being staked for city settlement lots and streets. There I dug the holes, cut forks for posts and set them and poles for the top, then placed the brush cover, there being no lumber. The railroad officers permitted me to seat this arbor with railroad ties, new ones just unloaded and down on the river where laborers had been camping. I found an empty 100 pound coffee box. . . . I used this for a pulpit and for conducting service the day of the opening.

Before the break of the opening day trains were coming in with passengers, bedding and baggage. By evening time, campfires and people crowded around the depot in vast numbers. There by lantern light that night, I preached to a mass of people and continued to do so for several days, also offering church fellowship to those becoming settled and remaining close enough for church fellowship. . . . It was under such conditions that Boston Avenue Methodist Church had to make its start, and I was happy to be with them.

LETTER FROM E.B. CHENOWETH TO DR. FRED CLINTON

THE CHENOWETHS
REV. EDGAR BENSON CHENOWETH
AND SUSAN ERVINE CHENOWETH
SHORTLY AFTER THEIR WEDDING.

Edgar Benson Chenoweth was only twenty-four years old when he drove a little spring wagon pulled by two western ponies over the mountains from Cortez, Colorado, to Indian Territory. With him were his wife, Susan Eleanor Ervine Chenoweth, almost twenty-three, and their infant son, Paul Duncan Chenoweth.

Edgar Chenoweth had been orphaned at a young age. He met Eleanor Ervine when he went to Kansas to live with his uncle Joe Hatcher, who was married to Eleanor's sister Lillian. Eleanor and Edgar were married July 15, 1891 and moved to Stewart, Colorado,

where he was the circuit preacher. The Reverend Chenoweth had an inheritance from his parents and invested it in two failing newspapers, the *Denver Dispatch,* and the *Rocky Mountain Methodist.* Both failed, and he went to preach in Cortez, Colorado. From there, Chenoweth answered the call to come to Indian Territory.

Because the opening of the Cherokeee Strip took place in September and the Vinita Conference was held two months later, there is some confusion about whether or not the family went to Vinita first. Perhaps the Chenoweths were first sent to the little Indian Territory village of Tulsa as a temporary assignment during the land run. The Cherokee Outlet was a 120,000 square-mile expanse of prairie to be opened for settlement at high noon on September 16, and Tulsa, some twenty miles from its southeastern corner, was the nearest town served by a railroad—a gathering place for people making the run. The Chenoweths arrived a few days before the run with no food and almost no money, to begin their ministry in the new territory. As Eleanor Chenoweth recalled sixty-two years later:

> *When we got to Tulsey, we had used up all our flour on that long trip. . . . We didn't have but fifteen cents because our allowance hadn't come in before we left. We needed a sack of flour most so that's what we tried to get credit for. . . . When Dad asked for credit [at the grocery store] to buy a sack of flour, the owner refused. A Mr. Graybeal, who was a clerk in the store, stepped forward and said, "Go ahead and get your sack of flour. I'll pay for it."*

Mrs. Chenoweth's memory was that the Reverend Chenoweth preached his first Tulsa sermons in the saloons. "Then we built . . . a brush arbor and held services there in the summertime." In November, during the meeting of the Indian Mission Conference at Vinita, the Reverend Chenoweth was officially given the challenging missionary assignment to establish the Methodist Episcopal Church South in the vicinity of Tulsa.

In the year 1893 Tulsa was more than the staked-out townsite described in Chenoweth's letter, but it was still a new settlement. The first public Christian worship service in the town had been held by a traveling preacher ten years earlier on the stoop of the Hall Brothers store. A Presbyterian mission was built in 1885 and a year later the "northern" Methodist Episcopal Church was established, later to be known as the First Methodist Church.

DOWNTOWN TULSA
TULSA IS SEEN AS IT LOOKED AT THE TIME THE METHODIST EPISCOPAL CHURCH SOUTH WAS ESTABLISHED.

**LOLA AND DONNA BREWER
1888.**

LOLA, AGE THIRTEEN, AND DONNA
BREWER, FIVE, ARE SHOWN PRIOR TO
THE BREWER FAMILY'S MOVE TO
TULSA. THE PICTURE WAS TAKEN IN
SPRINGFIELD, MISSOURI.

"When I arrived there in November 1893," the Reverend Chenoweth would later recall, "there was one small two-story frame hotel, one drug store, one barber shop (run by Sterling McAlister) one dressmaker and milliner shop (run by his sisters), one blacksmith shop, and the general stores of R.N. Bynum, Price & Gillette, Lynch Brothers, and the Bradys' store which was located on the north side of the railroad and was conducted by Tate Brady and his parents.

"The hotel also was on the north side, the depot on the east side of the road from the Bradys', all else was on the south side of the track. There were about thirty-five or forty families in or accessible to Tulsa. There was a mission of the Presbyterian Church."

Tate Brady's general merchandise store, which had been built in 1890, advertised "A Dollar's Worth of Honest Goods for a Dollar in Money." The story is told that on their very first night in Tulsa, the Chenoweths were eating dinner in the St. Elmo Hotel and the Reverend Chenoweth asked if there were any members of the Methodist Episcopal Church South in town. W.R. Wallace told him about the Brewer family, so he promptly went to visit them.

Dr. F.L. Brewer, his wife Mary, and daughters Lola, age eighteen, and Donna, eight, had come to Tulsa from Springfield, Missouri, shortly before the Chenoweths arrived. They had asked about a local Methodist Episcopal Church South, but since there were none, they put their letter in at the Methodist Episcopal Church "north," which was north of the Frisco tracks near Main.

The "north" and "south" designations had nothing to do with locations in the town. They indicated a division in the church resulting from a pre-Civil War dispute over slavery, a division into two separate denominations, which would outlast the slavery issue by many years.

When the Reverend Chenoweth talked to the Brewers, they were enthusiastic about helping him to organize a Tulsa church. They were generous, hospitable people, and took the Chenoweths into their home until they found a place to live, according to Lola Brewer. The Brewers gave the little church strong support in those early years.

Mrs. Chenoweth and Lola Brewer would later recall that the Chenoweths lived in a dugout at first, a pit with wood framing above ground. Lola Brewer said the dugout was on what would become North Cheyenne. The Reverend Chenoweth's account of that time differs significantly: "The only place I could find on arriving that I could rent to move into was a little 8' x 10' plain box shack one mile south of the depot on the riverbank in the Perryman Woods pasture. This I secured for one dollar per month. Here we moved and spent the winter and most of the first year."

He also wrote, "I had visited in most of the accessible homes and found Sterling McAlister and his two sisters (their father was a pastor in Missouri); the Bradys, Tate and his parents; and J.M.

Crutchfield and his wife, a Cherokee cattleman living half a mile northeast of the depot. Also the Forsythe brothers and their families—they were in teaming and contracting—and Noah Gregory, a Creek stockman, and his family who lived south of Red Fork. All these I found most approachable and anxious for our church. I proceeded to cultivate a general Sunday school spirit among them and their friends, and soon we were proud of our efforts, though limited for lack of house room and equipment."

Many early records on the church are incomplete or missing as keeping records was not the first priority in those hard early years. Thus there are no records which clearly state "these were the first members of the church."

Mrs. Chenoweth would recall years later that the church had seven founding members. Lola Brewer also remembered that seven people established the church, and she named them as: the Reverend and Mrs. Chenoweth, Dr. F.L. Brewer, Mrs. Brewer, Lola Brewer, and Mr. and Mrs. George Forsythe. Although the Reverend Chenoweth's official records from the time show that Lola Brewer did not move her certificate of membership to the church until October 1897 when her younger sister Donna became a member on profession of faith, she was apparently involved before she became an official member.

The little group she named, along with Noah Gregory, probably were the ones who met in the Presbyterian mission school building at what is now the southeast corner of Fourth and Boston to organize Tulsa's Methodist Episcopal Church South. Tulsa's pioneering merchant and ruling Presbyterian elder, J.M. Hall, later recalled attending that organizational meeting to lend his moral support to the southern Methodists. The new congregation continued meeting once a month in the Presbyterian Mission through that first winter.

Nor were the Presbyterians alone in giving them moral support and shelter. One of the treasured items in the archives at Boston Avenue Church is a poster, which is believed to date from December 1893, advertising an evening of entertainment to be held at the

DR. AND MRS. FRED L. BREWER
DR. AND MRS. BREWER WERE PIONEER MEMBERS OF THE METHODIST EPISCOPAL CHURCH SOUTH IN TULSA.

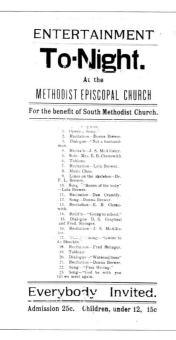

**"ENTERTAINMENT TONIGHT"
BULLETIN (ABOVE).**
PRINTED IN DECEMBER, 1893, THIS
BULLETIN ANNOUNCES AN EARLY
CHURCH BENEFIT.

**IDA BUCK CONAWAY AND
LOREN (LON) CONAWAY, SR.
(RIGHT)**

Methodist Episcopal Church "for the benefit of South Methodist Church." Featured on the program of songs, tableaus, and recitations were Donna, Lola, and Dr. F.L. Bewer; E.B. and Mrs. Chenoweth; J.S. McAllister; D.S. Graybeal; and Fred Stringer.

Along with the congregation at Tulsa, the Reverend Chenoweth established new churches at Duck Creek and Catoosa. To serve these three churches, he "rode the circuit." At the quarterly conference in December 1893, E.B. Chenoweth was recorded as P.C. (preacher in charge) of the Tulsa church. Noah G. Gregory was L.P. (local preacher), and was elected secretary. His "exhorter's license" was also renewed. The Reverend Chenoweth reported "no church organizations" at that time.

By February, 1894, seventeen dollars had been raised in the little church, and the Reverend Chenoweth was paid eleven dollars for the quarter. Dr. Brewer, a trustee, was elected district secretary for the coming year, and it was reported that $48.45 had been raised for a parsonage.

In May, 1894, the Reverend Chenoweth reported that Mrs. Ida Conaway and Mrs. Etta Chaney had joined the church in Tulsa and Mrs. Conaway's baby daughter, Juanita Bernice, was baptized during that quarter. Members raised $6.55 for the support of the ministry and twelve dollars for foreign missions. Ben Robinson and George Forsythe were stewards, and Forsythe was elected secretary and Sunday school superintendent. Robinson, Forsythe, and "Jno" (as John was often spelled in those times) Brown were elected delegates to the district conference. The pastor reported that the spiritual state of the church was encouraging.

Mrs. Conaway quickly became involved in the church, teaching a Sunday school class for young boys and serving as president of the Women's Parsonage and Home Mission Society. Her great-grandfather Isaac Buck and several uncles were Methodist ministers, so her church was important to her. Mrs. Conaway's husband, Loren Alroy Conaway, had come to Tulsa earlier to work on one of the largest ranches in the territory, the Mashed O Ranch owned by William E. Halsell. Halsell was a Texan married to a Texas girl of Cherokee descent, and their rock ranch house was located across Bird Creek from what later became Mohawk Park.

Conaway, usually called Lon, later became a lawman and a building contractor, and went back to Missouri to marry his childhood sweetheart, Ida Christine Buck. She was a gently reared young woman who had attended Cottey College, so her father was concerned about her coming to the wilderness of Indian Territory. Indeed life was hard, and little Juanita Conaway lived only four years. A second Conaway daughter would die in 1901 at age two.

Tulsa and the future Boston Avenue Church would grow up together, for the town was ready to boom just when the church was founded. Besides the influence of the historic land run, development of the railroad from Kansas to Texas and from Missouri as far as Sapulpa had encouraged the growth of Tulsa and several other small white settlements in the vacinity.

The year of the church's founding was also the year the federal government began to liquidate Indian tribal ownership of lands in Indian Territory where Tulsa was located. As the government closed

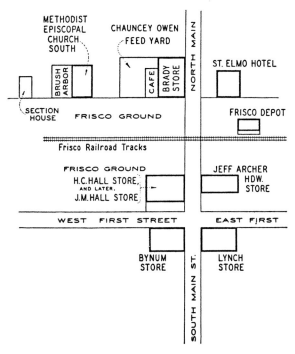

PLAT OF TULSA, I. T., 1893, SHOWING LOCATION OF METHODIST EPISCOPAL CHURCH, SOUTH

Sketch by Lon R. Stansbery and Fred S. Clinton
Delineation by Walter L. Perryman

TULSA, 1893

THIS PLAT OF TULSA SHOWS THE LOCATION OF THE CHURCH AND OTHER BUILDINGS NEAR THE RAILROAD TRACKS.

out the affairs of the Creeks, Cherokees, and other tribes who owned Tulsa and the surrounding land, the Indians were gradually allotted farms according to the number of people in the family. White settlers soon organized to promote statehood for Indian Territory and Oklahoma Territory.

The opening of the Cherokee Strip had brought many white settlers into the region, families interested in building their homes in and around Tulsa. The Reverend Chenoweth seems to have been tireless in his efforts to develop a ministry to these settlers and to bring them into the church. "One of my first public services I performed in Tulsa was to conduct the funeral service of Brother J.M. Crutchfield, which was an opening wedge of friendship thereafter," Chenoweth later wrote. Crutchfield's widow Josie joined Chenoweth's congregation at Duck Creek in the first part of 1894, then soon transferred to Tulsa where she became an active member of the church.

When the cold winter of 1893-4 was over, the little church began to make progress. "During the spring and summer of 1894 we worked along as best we could until we finally succeeded in raising enough to buy a lot on the north side of the railroad west of Brady's store. Then we procured posts and timbers and built a brush arbor which we seated with borrowed lumber on railroad ties. Here held a very happy and successful meeting as well as our regular and other services," the Reverend Chenoweth reported. In September 1894, J.B. Sledge was elected secretary of the little Tulsa congregation, and the preacher in charge was paid thirty dollars.

A 60' x 100' lot valued at twenty dollars was donated to the church. It was located a block and a half from the Frisco Depot on the north side of the right of way and west. The members secured enough box lumber and other materials that by September, erection of a real church building had begun and contracts had been made to the amount of $25.70. "We feel confident of an early completion of our church," they said.

Miss Margaret Chenoweth, the Chenoweth's older daughter, later reported that when this church was being built, the walls were up and the roof was going on when the donors decided they wanted their land back. They threatened bodily injury to the Reverend Chenoweth and the men of the congregation who were working on it if one more nail was driven. The others stopped, but Chenoweth was determined. Members of the newly-organized Masonic Lodge, bearing guns, stood guard while the minister finished putting the roof on by himself.

During the last week of December, 1894, the *Tulsa Democrat* reported that "Brother Chenoweth thinks the church building will be completed by February if the weather is not too inclement." This little church, later known as the "box church," was a plain 32' x 40'

THE BRUSH ARBOR
THE ILLUSTRATION IS AN ARTIST'S
CONCEPTION OF HOW THE BRUSH
ARBOR IS LIKELY TO HAVE
LOOKED.

building with three windows on each side and a door at one end. The pulpit was at the end opposite the door. Mrs. Ida Conaway painted the glass windows and the glass in the door, and the building was pronounced "adequate for all time to come" by the pastor and building committee.

Meanwhile, the work of adding two more rooms to the parsonage on North Cheyenne was underway, with lumber purchased in the amount of $70. Hauling and laying stone foundation cost $9.90. The trustees and building committee estimated that the parsonage alone when completed would be worth $350, or $450 for parsonage and lot.

The Reverend Chenoweth built small chairs for the tots in the nursery and a cradle for "noisy babies." Mrs. Chenoweth's sister Mrs. Lillian Irvine Hatcher was the first school teacher when classes began in the little church.

Later the Reverend Chenoweth related, "Most of the time I was at Tulsa I had regular appointments once a month also at Red Fork, and at the National School Chapel at Sapulpa. I also held services and protracted meetings at numerous other places about the country using brush arbors and school houses as the settlements were growing up. All these associations continued a constant feeder to Tulsa and the work there."

Lola Brewer later wrote, "Brother Chenoweth had to ride the

circuit (or walk part of it when the Arkansas River was ugly). Red Fork was one of his charges, and many times he walked the Frisco Bridge to his charge and back at night, which was a little dangerous in the early days. But he never faltered and it is largely due to his devotion to his work that we as a church had a good beginning."

Tulsa was a busy town in 1894. Robert E. Lynch built the town's first masonry building, a general store, on the southeast corner of First and Main streets from stone quarried in Dawson, later to be part of north Tulsa. Lanterns, wood and metal buckets, boots, cups, canned food, dishes, potatoes, and other essentials of frontier life were for sale in his store. In December, three dollars were reported paid to the preacher in charge. There was as yet no Epworth League or Sunday school. Chenoweth reported that the "state of the church is not as good spiritually as we would like to see it." One infant, Lula Miller, was baptized that quarter.

By March, 1895, the congregation had moved into the box church, and had seven Sunday school officers and teachers and thirty scholars. They spent $2.50 on Sunday school literature and the preacher in charge was paid twenty-eight dollars for the quarter. Miss Julia and Miss Emma McAlister were received by letter.

In 1895, the government asked the Reverend Chenoweth to leave his charge and conduct the Eucha School for Indians at Sapulpa. "They offered eighteen hundred dollars a year," Margaret Chenoweth recalled, "which was much more than the three hundred to four hundred dollars he was getting from the church. But he persuaded a friend, Mr. N.G. Gregory (likely Noah Gregory, the first local preacher of the church) to take the assignment. Father's reasoning was that Mr. Gregory was better qualified than he because he spoke two tribal languages as well as English. Father had only Greek and Latin."

THE MEAT MARKET, 1893

THIS PHOTO IS LABELED "UNCLE BARTON CHENOWETH AT THE MEAT MARKET."

By June, the widowed Josie Crutchfield had transferred to Tulsa and a "Sister Prewitt" also was received by letter. The pastor and J.B. Sledge, trustee, reported one church and one parsonage, with the value of each being about five hundred dollars and an indebtedness of forty-three dollars on both properties. The title papers were in Lynch's safe and recorded in the U.S. Court in Muskogee.

An Epworth League was finally started, with twelve pledged members, and Sunday school attendance was up to thirty-five. Trustees at that time were G.R. French, who had been received by vows that quarter, John Cox, E.B. Chenoweth, and George Bullette. Bullette, a grocer, owned a large home on North Norfolk.

Like the church, the little town was growing. By 1895 Tulsa had thirty-eight businesses operating under trader's licenses, Indian businessmen who paid no licenses, and some others who "dodged their obligation." One of the businesses was the Frisco Meat Market, which featured deer, raccoon, rabbits, quail, and prairie chicken, all hung in front of the store for the customers to view and make their selections. There were three weekly newspapers: the *Tulsa Review,* the *Indian Republican* (which would become the *Tulsa World*), and the *Tulsa Democrat* (later to become the *Tulsa Tribune*).

Most of this growth was taking place south of the railroad tracks. As the Reverend Chenoweth would recall years later, ". . . the more approachable and beautiful south side . . . was rapidly building up and in the course of a short period we felt we were not where we could keep up with the movements. . . ." Thus, the box church was moved south of the tracks and up the hill to a "more promising location . . . one block east and another south of the old depot."

In 1895 the Reverend Chenoweth was secretary of the Indian Mission Conference Sunday school committee and served on the district records committee. The records committee that year was critical of the condition of the journals kept by the pastors, noting that there were blotches, things were crowded together, and they were not neat. Much of the information about those early days comes from Chenoweth's own quarterly records, which were carefully written in beautiful script, obviously with an old steel or quill pen.

In later years, the Reverend E.B. Chenoweth's family would report that he wore out several Bibles during his ministry, and that they never saw him without the bookmark in his Bible saying "No Cross—No Crown." This motto was an appropriate one for a pastor in the Indian Mission Conference, for times were far from easy on American's frontier.

"Some of our preachers stand like lone pickets on duty. Others are engaged in work as purely missionary as any in China, Japan, or darkest Africa," said the chairman of the Indian Mission Conference in 1895. "All things considered, we think the Indian Mission Conference is on safe and rising ground spiritually."

THE HARD EARLY YEARS

The Reverend Webster Full - 1896-1897
The Reverend J.M. Porter - 1898-1899
The Reverend A.S.J. Haygood - 1899-1900
The Reverend J.M. Porter - 1900

Pastors in the Methodist Episcopal Church South in the 1890s were moved at least every three years, and at the Indian Mission Conference in 1896, the Reverend Chenoweth was transferred from Tulsa. In a letter to Dr. John A. Rice in 1927, E.B. Chenoweth poignantly tells of his experience at the conference of 1896.

DID THE BISHOP FORGET THE PREACHER?

It was at the conclusion of the Sunday evening service bringing to an end the annual conference presided over by Bishop Key of Texas in 1896. The Bishop had announced the appointments for the pastors both new and old, of the newly organized, rapidly building Oklahoma conference that had so recently been struggling along as the old Indian Mission Conference of the ME Church South. The Bishop expressed to the audience his gratitude at the success of the past year and his best wishes and earnest hope and prayer for a most successful new one to all.

Throughout the service on the back seat of the neat little frame church sat a young preacher with his wife and their two small children. He had driven a pony team and buggy all the way from Tulsa where he had been stationed the three preceding years, for as yet the railroad only reached as far as Sapulpa. And three years then being the "time limit," he had come expecting to be moved.

But where? At an earlier hour of the conference session he had been elected and the Bishop had ordained him an Elder. But now the last moments of the conference session have arrived and the Bishop has announced, actually "read out" the appointments of the pastors and churches such as Dr. T.J. Brewer, Dr. J.M. Gross, J.M. Porter and all the rest . . . and has never called that man's name.

Oh, what will happen for he is forgotten, and with no place to go and no money and the ponies getting old, and the harness and buggy about to fall down and even their clothes getting shabby and worn. What, oh what, will he do?

Under such rending meditations the Bishop continued by

saying something like this: "Now, brethren, let us all thank God and take courage and the victory shall be ours." The congregation will now stand and receive the benediction by El Reno Station, E.B. Chenoweth.". . . The Benediction was then pronounced.

The conference report indicated a 1,616 net gain in membership during the past year. Tulsa had twenty-five white members and no Indian members.

The Reverend Webster Full was appointed at the conference to take charge of the Tulsa church. Upon coming to Tulsa in late 1896, he reported sadly that, "some of our members are worldly minded." He was paid seventeen dollars for the quarter.

The education report given at the conference stated that there were three hundred thousand white people in the Indian Territory without any public school system and few religious or church schools, with only medium attention being paid to education by the Indian governments. "There is a field of usefulness open for our church," the report concluded.

A Creek neighborhood school had operated in Tulsa as early as 1880, and a subscription school was opened in 1883 for the settlers' children. In 1884, the Presbyterian Mission School was built on a small hill at what would later be Fourth and Boston in downtown Tulsa, and it was in this building that the church members had met before the construction of the box church. By late 1896, the church was ready to return the favor. In January of 1897, the trustees of the Methodist Episcopal Church South voted to allow Miss Etta Moreland to teach school in the box church for the space of three months, free of charge.

The short "lease" on the building may have been due to the fact that the box church was no longer deemed adequate for the congregation. At the last 1896 conference, Mrs. Josie Crutchfield, Dr. J.S. McAlister, and Mrs. Ida Conaway were appointed an estimating committee to determine the cost of a new church building.

On April 12, 1897, the trustees met in the parsonage to consider the matter of a new building. A motion was made that Lon Conaway be appointed a committee of one to sell the "box church" building with any help the trustees might render him. Josie Crutchfield, Webster Full, and Emma McAlister were appointed a committee to procure a lot for a new church building, and Mrs. Crutchfield, Miss McAlister, and Mr. Lon Conaway were appointed a committee on solicitation.

The quarterly conference passed several resolutions in July of 1897 to smooth the way for the new building. First, the trustees were instructed by the quarterly conference to collect the forty dollars due the church from Brother George M. Forsythe, and to apply it on a

THE BOX CHURCH BUILDING SCHOOL, 1896

THE REV. CHENOWETH AND SCHOOLTEACHER MISS MINNE COGSWELL ARE PICTURED WITH THE STUDENTS WHO ATTENDED SCHOOL AT THE BOX CHURCH.

mortgage of fifty dollars (due and unpaid), held by Mrs. Josie Crutchfield against the lots on which the parsonage and box church stood. They also resolved that the trustees collect by subscription the remaining ten dollars and satisfy the mortgage as soon as possible. Second, the trustees were authorized to sell the lumber purchased for pews for not less than fifteen dollars and to use that money for chairs to be used in the present church until a new church was erected.

Lola Brewer reported in later years that she and her father talked with T.E. Smiley about buying the fifty-foot lot where the Robinson Hotel would later be built. But he wanted a dollar a foot for it, which was too much. They then went to see George B. Perryman, a prosperous Creek rancher, about some land where a church could be built. He was very generous and offered them all the land from Main to Detroit, and from Fifth to Eighth streets—free. "But the rest of the church would not have it," Lola Brewer recalled years later. "They said it was too far out of town, under the hill, and strangers wouldn't know it was there."

A fire in mid-December, 1897, raged through Tulsa, destroying three masonry buildings and twelve wooden structures, including Tulsa Banking Company, the city's first bank. (Luckily, the vault was saved.) The fire alarm in those days was a series of gunshots, and fires were fought with a bucket brigade. It would not be until 1900 that the first fire wagon for the town was purchased and a volunteer fire department organized.

An event that was to change the area forever also occurred in 1897. The first commercial oil well in Oklahoma was brought in near Bartlesville, fifty-two miles to the north of Tulsa, luring fortune seekers from all over the country into the territory.

Dr. Fred S. Clinton, a name which would become well known both in church and oil circles, brought his Georgia bride to Tulsa that year. She was the former Jane Carroll Heard, and they lived for a while with his mother in the ornate family home on a hilltop at Half Circle S Ranch in Red Fork. Mother Clinton, Louise Atkins Clinton, was half Creek Indian and half white, and Charles, Fred's father who had died at age forty, was white. Fred was a tall, blue-eyed blonde in spite of his strong Indian heritage.

There were four children in the Clinton family; Fred, Lee, Paul, and Vera. Lee also married a Georgia girl, Susan Merrill, and Vera married J.H. McBirney. Paul, who would become a real estate man, married Fan Knight. All would be long-time members of the Methodist Episcopal Church South except Vera. J.H. McBirney's father was a Methodist minister in Ireland, and they would become staunch members of the Methodist Episcopal Church (First Methodist) in Tulsa.

In 1897, the Reverend J.M. Porter was assigned to Tulsa. The official roll of the 1897-1898 conference listed as trustees the Reverend J.M. Porter, preacher in charge; R.R. Roberts, Guy Allen, Ida Conaway, and Josie Crutchfield, stewards; Emma McAlister and Julia Smith, stewards and trustees; Mary Melissa Brewer and George Forsythe, trustees; and R. R. Smith, trustee.

When he arrived in Tulsa, Porter found a congregation moving forward with plans for building a new church and improving the parsonage. In January of 1898, he reported that the Women's Parsonage and Home Mission Society had raised ninety-eight dollars during the last year for the purpose of buying a church lot in a more central location in town. "My predecessor, just after leaving the conference and before I reached the work, withdrew fifty dollars of this amount to pay off a mortgage which Josie Crutchfield held against the present church and parsonage lots, and a three dollar debt said to have been on the parsonage foundation."

Porter, obviously unaware of the resolutions passed at the July '97 conference authorizing these payments, continued rather heatedly, "There is not the scratch of a pen, that we can find, for

L. L. Hall, The Photographer, TULSA, I. T.

authority in diverting this money from its legitimate channel, or the purpose for which it was raised. Not having enough to purchase a lot, and the parsonage in need of enlarging and fixing up, the Women's Parsonage and Home Mission Society decided to use the remaining forty-five dollars on hand towards the said parsonage improvements."

"With this amount in hand," he continued, "we began the work of adding two more rooms 12' x 14' to the present [parsonage] building. We collected the forty dollars G.M. Forsythe was due the church on old lots sold him, and applied this amount on the lumber bill. Now we have a very good four-room house, nicely papered and painted, and well worth five hundred dollars. We hope to begin operations for a new church soon."

In early 1898, the Sunday school had seven officers and

teachers and thirty-three pupils on the roll. "The Senior Epworth League disbanded or quit work sometime last year and we have not been able to get it reorganized," reported the Reverend Porter. "The new year finds our people, what few we have, living upright lives and ready to cooperate in the minister's work. Nothing shall be left undone by us in furthering the church's interests along every line during the year."

In March, the Reverend Porter reported that they had moved the box church. This move is believed to have been to a lot on Second Street between Cincinnati and Detroit. The Epworth League had been reorganized and fifty were on the roll in the Sunday school. Mr. George Perryman gave the church ten dollars and Mrs. Josie Crutchfield contributed five dollars, leaving $36.75 due on the parsonage.

Miss Emma McAlister, who had been elected Sunday school superintendent in January, received words of praise from the Reverend Porter. "The superintendent has been faithful to her trust during the quarter. She did the proper thing not long ago and took unto herself a husband. Of course, she will still go forward with the work."

"Our Sunday school is doing very good work," he reported. "When our Baptist friends pulled off from us to organize in their new building, our numbers were depleted considerably for a few Sundays, but our forces rallied, and now our attendance is as good if not better than before." The Baptists, who were just organizing what would become the First Baptist Church, apparently had attended the Methodist Sunday school while their new building was under construction nearby.

Our Brother in Red was the official publication of the Indian Mission Conference in Indian and Oklahoma territories. In a March 1, 1898, article in that publication, the Reverend Porter wrote, "We are moving along very well in our new charge, all things considered. Have done much needed work on the parsonage and am planning for a new church building. Not much can be accomplished here without one.

"A good brother to whom I wrote for advice in building, etc., has written me to get my members saved and then we could build without help, etc., etc. We have only twenty members now, all of these women and children but two.

"Of course, we need a revival not so much to get the members saved but to get some members who are able to do something."

The Reverend Porter reported that regular Sunday services were much better attended than during the quarter before, and that George Forsythe and his family, early members of the church, had moved away from Tulsa.

The congregation had not exactly outgrown the little box

church which had been pronounced "adequate for all time to come" when they finished it just four years earlier. What had changed was Tulsa and the image church members had of their town. A box church was adequate for an Indian mission village, but not for the city Tulsa was becoming. In 1898, "Tulsey town" was officially incorporated as the City of Tulsa, when L.M. Poe, J.M. Hall, and Dr. S.G. Kennedy drove a buggy to Muskogee and brought back the new city charter.

Louis Milton Poe, a lawyer from Arkansas, had moved his family to Tulsa earlier that year. He and his wife Lou Lane Poe would eventually have a large family, with five boys and one girl who grew up in the church.

A building committee was elected in March, 1898, made up of the Reverend Porter, Dr. Brewer, and R.R. Roberts, with the power to dispose of the box church for not less than one hundred dollars and to do whatever they thought proper to secure a new church in a central location. The box church building was sold sometime in the next few months, but the efforts to secure a new church stalled out.

"We are moving along very well with our work here, all things considered," the Reverend Porter wrote in *Our Brother in Red* in July. "Have been tussling with an attack of malaria for over two weeks. Trust though to be alright soon. Good deal of sickness here about and some deaths. The shortness of the wheat and oat crop we fear will preclude the possibility of our building the new church this year."

THE BOX CHURCH

THE BOX CHURCH IS SHOWN HERE AFTER IT WAS MOVED AND WAS NO LONGER IN USE BY THE CONGREGATION.

He reported that the church had bought and paid for a bell at a cost of $55.25, had a well drilled, and made other improvements on the church and parsonage amounting to $22.80.

As Tulsa developed from a village to a "city," members of the church were developing some cosmopolitan tastes in entertainment which didn't always meet with their pastors' approval. The Reverend Porter's concern for the spiritual state of his flock was evident in July, 1898, when he reported, "A month ago this report would have been different. I thought up to that time that we were getting along pretty well. But since then our people have been taking in the *shows, races and dances . . . and more especially the stomp dance* of late, and hence I cannot make a favorable report at this time. Of course, spiritually minded people do not love these things."

Indeed, with no church structure to call its own, church morale seems to have reached a low ebb that summer. By September 1898, the Sunday school had been suspended because there was no place to meet. "The selling of the old shack of a church building has kind of demoralized things somewhat," the pastor said, but his optimism was unquenchable. "We can have a first class school just as soon as we get a church building. We now have a good bell, organ, 28 benches, and a comfortable four-room parsonage. A new church building will put us in the lead here."

The Reverend Porter was moved the following year before he could see his optimistic predictions come true. At the Indian Mission Conference in 1899, the Reverend A.S.J. Haygood was assigned to the M.E. Church South in Tulsa. It was also reported that Webster Full, the second pastor at the Tulsa church, had withdrawn from the ministry and from membership in the church.

Even though there still was no church building, the church managed to attract some of Tulsa's leading citizens as members. Wyatt Tate Brady joined the church during the first quarter of 1899, as did Dr. W.M. Wilson, Eugene A. Wilkinson, and Mrs. Flora Rollman. Tate Brady would be the first "Mr. Tulsa" a few years later. Brady and Dr. Wilson would also become brothers-in-law in 1904, when Wilson married Susan Electra Davis, the sister of Brady's wife Rachel. Rachel and Susan were daughters of John Davis, a citizen of the Cherokee Nation.

DR. W. M. WILSON

Dr. Washington Milner Wilson had not been in Tulsa long when he joined the church. He had stopped in town only to wait until the mud dried out, not intending to stay. He was from a large Georgia family whose plantation had suffered at the hands of General Sherman's troops during the Civil War. As a small boy, his job was to go into the fields and pick up cannon balls so that the field could be plowed. He had been apprenticed to an itinerant dentist and traveled with him on horseback from one southern town to another. When the dentist left to join the forces of Teddy Roosevelt in Cuba, Wilson bought his equipment and won a horse and buggy in a raffle.

Having heard about Indian Territory, he started toward one of the bigger towns—Okmulgee or Muskogee. He was operating his dentist office out of the back of the buggy and looking for a town which didn't have a good dentist firmly entrenched.

Wilson liked Tulsa and stayed, joining the church and becoming active in the community. He started the first music store and the first laundry and was part owner in the first sawmill. He liked real estate and was involved in all kinds of businesses. But he was devoted to his church. When it was still very small, he would pump the organ, take up the collection, then hurry to add his tenor voice to the choir.

One story that Dr. Wilson told about Tulsa's muddy streets involved a very prominent lady whom he was too proper to name. At that time he had an office over the Strand Theater, and was standing at the window one day watching this lady pick her way down the muddy, sticky street, holding her long skirts up out of the mire. Just as she was stepping across a particularly big puddle, the drawstring on her bloomers broke and down they came around her ankles. There was the usual contingent of loafers standing around on the street corners, and Dr. Wilson wondered what in the world she would do. Life in Tulsa had apparently taught her to meet difficult situations with grace and ingenuity. She calmly stepped out of the bloomers, daintily pushed them down into the mud puddle out of sight, and continued serenely on her way.

L.M. Poe was added to the church building committee in 1899, and soon would become Sunday school superintendent. By March 15, 1900, the church was hard pressed for money, and the authority was granted the board of trustees to sell the parsonage to forward the church building.

The Reverend Haygood transferred to the New Mexico Conference in 1900 and J. M. Porter returned to pastor the Tulsa church. This time, however, the Tulsa church had to share his services with churches in Sapulpa and Bristow. On Porter's return he found the state of the church worse than it had been when he left the year before. In August, 1900, he reported that the congregation had only twenty-six members, and had been shut out of the Opera House where they had been meeting because one of the young people turned over a lamp and nearly set the building on fire.

"Our people are not only disorganized but completely discouraged. They have had a station preacher so long, it is hard for them to get accustomed to every other Sunday for preaching, consequently it is a difficult matter to interest them in the attendance upon the measures of grace." Still optimistic, Porter went on to report, "We trust soon to see a change in all these things. We have some good people, and with a creditable church building can be in a short time in the forefront of our Master's work."

Apparently the parsonage wasn't sold, because it was reported in October that the congregation had a parsonage in Tulsa valued at six hundred dollars with a debt of forty-four dollars, a lot for a church at the same place which cost three hundred dollars, and a stone foundation costing $367. "The title papers are as perfect as such documents can be in this Territory at the present time," was the cryptic report.

The Brick Church
The Reverend C.W. Myatt - 1901-1903

The Reverend C. W. Myatt was sent to Tulsa in 1901 to build a church and he spared no effort. He spent many an afternoon stationed in Dr. W.M. Wilson's dentist office, inquiring of every person who entered if they would like to contribute toward building a church. He made fifty pastoral visits in the quarter following his arrival, and, while no new people joined the congregation, he felt the spiritual state of the church was improved.

In 1901 the city was laid out and streets were named by a surveyor employed by the federal townsite commission. The townsite included 654.58 acres with a total valuation of $107,173.30.

Dr. Fred Clinton and his brother Lee, who would be vital members of the church for years, were busy helping build the growing community. Dr. Clinton cared for patients all over the area and invested in various business ventures. Lee Clinton, who worked at the bank, owned the ferry that crossed the Arkansas River about where the Eleventh Street bridge would later be built.

On June 12, 1901, Lee Clinton's ferry operator came running into the bank where Lee worked shouting, "There's two crazy men down at the ferry, dancing and yelling. They're saying that they've struck oil!" And they had. Dr. Fred Clinton and his partner Dr. J.C.W. Bland had struck oil in Red Fork, four miles west of Tulsa. The lease on which they drilled was owned by Bland's half-Creek wife, Sue, and they named the well the Sue Bland.

Clinton and Bland's gusher brought men streaming in, searching for black gold. By June 25, according to a report in the *Kansas City Star,* all roads leading to Red Fork were full of horses and wagons bringing gamblers, promoters, speculators, lawyers, and even fortune tellers—but "not a geologist in the lot." Red Fork was soon known as "one of the vilest spots in the territory."

Dr. W.M. Wilson was elected secretary at the October 7, 1901, quarterly conference of the Tulsa and Bristow charge, and he and A.W. Wilhite, F.M. Hines, Mrs. Josie Crutchfield, and Lon Conaway were elected stewards for the coming year. The board of trustees was discharged and L.M. Poe, W.T. Brady, Dr. W.M. Wilson, F.M. Hines, A.W. Wilhite, Mrs. Josie Crutchfield, and Jay Forsythe made up the new board.

By unanimous vote of the quarterly conference the board of trustees of the Tulsa church was authorized to borrow money to pay the debt on the church and also to complete payment on the bell "after they had made thorough canvass and raised what they could on said amount, and they are also authorized to secure the money by any kind of ties on the church as seems best in the judgement of the board of trustees," the report stated.

The autumn of 1901 found the Reverend Myatt rejoicing, "We are devoutly thankful to report the spiritual state of our church at Tulsa good. We have had a gracious revival conducted by Brother John B. Andrews of Siloam Springs, Arkansas. There was over one hundred professions during the meeting and between seventy-five and one hundred united with the different churches."

Indeed, Myatt's efforts and the revival seem to have given the Tulsa church new life. A lot at Second and Cincinnati facing north and west was purchased from Pat Coyne, and construction on a brick church building began in 1901. By the quarterly conference in November of 1901, the Reverend Myatt recorded that there were two societies (churches) in the charge (Tulsa and Bristow), two houses of worship, no parsonages, and ninety-three members. The *Tulsa Democrat* reported in December that windows for the new Southern Methodist Church had arrived and that services could be held when they were put in.

"Our Sunday school is doing fairly well considering the

unfinished condition of our house of worship," the Reverend Myatt said in February of 1902. "We have not been able to have regular preaching and prayer meetings, but hope to finish the church and have it nicely furnished and then we believe will do well on all lines." It was reported that the church had opera folding chairs and the largest audience room of any church or building in town except the Opera House.

The sale of Tulsa city lots began in 1902, enabling people to have valid deeds to their property. The city could then levy taxes on residences and establishments to raise funds for civic improvements and plan for the future.

Lon Stansbery, a member of the church from these early years of the new century who owned and operated the Main Street Buggy, Wagon, and Farm Implement Store, was a smiling, plump man, a favorite in Tulsa. Years later, he would delight in telling stories about some of the early-day real estate dealings, even those in which he didn't come out on top. "I remember the first piece of property I bought in Tulsa was the entire block where the Santa Fe Freight office now stands. I paid ten dollars for it and slipped it to Dr. W.M. Wilson for twenty-five dollars. I felt like I had put one over on the doctor. However, he paid me with a city warrant, and I found the city had no money. So, in reality, the doctor handed me one."

Lee Clinton helped establish and then managed the Tulsa stockyards. Lee and his wife, Susan, and their son, Walton, moved to a one and a half-story house at Fifth and Houston where the state office building would sit in later years. Considered out in the country at that time, their home had a windmill and gas lights and they kept chickens and a cow. Walton would later recall hitching up the horses to drive into town to church on Sunday mornings. He also had his own cowpony named John L. which he rode at every opportunity, even on Sunday afternoons when his parents rode in the buggy. Watching the passenger trains come in was a big thing for small boys in those days.

The Sunday school had an average attendance of fifty by June of 1902, and the Reverend Myatt was paid $55.85 for the previous quarter. F.M. Hines and Lon Conaway were named stewards in August of 1902, and by February of 1903 the Reverend Myatt reported that the "spiritual state and condition of the church is some better now than at the first of the present quarter. We have some members that are faithful and true to God and His cause, and others who do not seem to think anything is required of them except to look after their own affairs."

THE BRICK CHURCH

A Junior Epworth League was organized in 1903. The Reverend Myatt said, "I think it will be a great power for good in this church." Mrs. Lee Clinton, Biron Carpenter, T.S. and Mrs. Neves, Mrs. Emmaly Dickerson, George M. Dickerson, and the Inhuffs, W.A., Nellie, Mrs. Etta, and Charlie, were received by letter.

The three-story Brady Hotel, built of brick, was completed in 1902 at Archer and Main. Tate Brady and some of the other town leaders began working in 1903 to get a second railroad into the town. The Katy Railroad had done a survey that took the route eight miles out of town, but Brady and his group had their own survey done, going through town, of course. They raised a bonus of twelve thousand dollars for the railroad to provide the right of way and induce them to change the route. It worked, and Tulsa's business leaders who had organized to bring in the railroad turned their energies toward boosting the town as a city with a boundless future.

Church and City Grow

The Reverend A.M. Brannon - 1903-1905
The Reverend J.H. Ball - 1906-1908

The Reverend A.M. Brannon became the Tulsa church's preacher in charge in November 1903. Upon his arrival at "the work," as pastors called their charges, the Reverend Brannon reported that the church had 111 members and one house of worship valued at four thousand dollars. He said the one Sunday school was doing fairly good work, and that both the Senior and Junior Epworth Leagues were very promising. He asked that the "Brethren pray that we may attain to higher heights in the Christian graces."

L.M. Poe, an active member of the church, was elected mayor of Tulsa in 1903. During his term as mayor, he was severely criticized for permitting a cemetery to be established at Eleventh and Peoria, because it was "so far out of town." He would also become the first federal judge of Tulsa and Pawnee Counties.

In February, the preacher in charge was paid $11.60 for the previous quarter and reported that the Sunday school was constantly growing in interest and numbers. "We think that we soon will have the best school in the district," the Reverend Brannon reported, and he had another goal for his flock. "Our aim and prayer is a gracious revival that will be felt in every home."

During the next six months, several new members would join the church who would forever change its history and that of Tulsa. Among them were Dr. and Mrs. Fred Clinton, Mr. and Mrs. J.R. Cole, Jr., and C.C. Cole.

J.R. Cole, Jr. and C.C. Cole were two of nine children of a Texas family. Their father, James Reid Cole, was one of the first presidents of what would become Texas A & M University. J.R. had gotten married in Oklahoma City the previous year, then moved to Tulsa. The couple spent the first nights at the Alcorn Hotel at First and Boston, but soon moved to the Kennedy House at Fourth and Boston, where they paid thirty dollars a month.

The five-story First National Bank building, which would boast Tulsa's first elevator, was begun in 1904. Meanwhile, Dr. Wilson sold his laundry and machinery to the Codrey brothers. Dr. Wilson also got married that year to Susan Electra Davis, sister of another church member, Mrs. Tate Brady. Sadly, Mrs. Wilson would live only seven

L.M. Poe, 1903 (LEFT)

Poe, an active member of the church, was elected mayor of Tulsa in 1903.

C.C. Cole (RIGHT)

C. C. Cole was yet another pioneer of the church in Tulsa. He joined the Methodist Episcopal Church South in 1903.

years after the birth of their only daughter, Julia.

Along with Tulsa's commercial development came an interest in culture and the arts, and the women of the church were in the forefront of the movement to establish cultural organizations in the community. Jane Heard Clinton and nine other women, all musicians, formed the Hyechka Club in 1904 to develop music appreciation in the community. The name is the Creek generic term for music. It was the first of many arts and civic groups to be organized by Jane Clinton.

By October 1904 the little church was well established, and the Reverend Brannon reported that its Junior Epworth League was doing good work, and the Sunday school was excellent. Twenty-eight people had been received that quarter. L.M. Poe was elected to the board of trustees, and Mrs. S.M. Latimer joined the church in late 1904. She would remain a member until her death in 1920.

"Our whole aim and prayer is for a real Holy Ghost revival. We hope to make this the most prosperous year of any in the history of the church," the Reverend Brannon said. J.R. Cole, Jr., was named Sunday school superintendent in January 1905, and by May there were more than two hundred enrolled in Sunday school.

Mr. and Mrs. J.D. Hagler joined the church that October. Don Hagler and his partners had given the town a major boost in January of 1904 with the building of a toll bridge connecting Tulsa with the oil fields across the Arkansas River in Red Fork. Tulsa and Red Fork were rivals, and neither had wanted to fund the bridge. Hagler, M.L. Baird, and George T. Williamson had raised fifty thousand dollars and built the toll bridge, hanging a sign above it that read, "They said we couldn't do it, but we did!" Kate Hagler would be a member of the church's far-sighted building committee in the 1920s.

The quarterly report of May, 1905, shows other notable additions to the church's membership. They included Mrs. A.E. Archer, Mable Archer, James Archer, and Mrs. G.W. Mowbray. Mrs. Mowbray was the wife of the mayor of Tulsa, a former minister at the other Methodist church. Mrs. Annie Archer was the Mowbrays' daughter, widow of pioneer Tulsa merchant Jeff Archer, for whom Archer Street is named.

The Reverend and Mrs. Mowbray had come from England, moving to Tulsa in 1888 to take over the pastorate of the struggling new Methodist Episcopal Church. In December of that year, when shots rang out interrupting a Christmas program at their church, Mrs. Mowbray restored order by going up and down the aisles, holding out her apron and demanding that all pistols be dropped into it. She laid the assortment on the rostrum, to be reclaimed after the service. In 1894, the Mowbrays were pastoring the Methodist church in Stillwater when Jeff Archer was killed by an exploding gunpowder keg in his store. The Reverand Mowbray had resigned from the ministry shortly after the accident, so he and Mrs. Mowbray could return to Tulsa to help their widowed daughter rebuild and operate the Archer store.

Mrs. Mowbray and the Archers were no doubt motivated to switch Methodist churches in 1905 due to the fact that First Methodist had just decided to build at Fifth and Boulder, moving that church from the north side of the railroad tracks to the south. The Archer family lived on the north side of the tracks, and, according to historians at Centenary Methodist Church, they and some forty other Methodists living on the north side, "were anxious to organize a Sunday School on the North side so that their children would not have to cross the tracks and wade through the mud to get to Sunday School."

On November 22, 1905, the Ida E. Glenn Number One blew in, the oil well owned by Robert Galbreath and Frank Chesley. This was the foundation of the great Glenn Pool, which would have more than five hundred wells by statehood and eventually boast more than five thousand. The businessmen of Tulsa were determined that their town would be the center for the oil industry. Sapulpa, Muskogee, and other towns were larger, but the Tulsans were more determined.

To encourage oil field workers to live in Tulsa, the civic leaders got the Frisco railroad to run a special train called "Coal Oil Johnny" that left Tulsa early in the morning and went through Sapulpa to

Okmulgee letting workers off. In the evening, it picked them up and returned them to Tulsa. A restaurant across from the railroad station called the "Pig's Ear" was popular with oil field workers, and W.N. Robinson's three story hotel advertised good meals and a bathtub. For those not staying in a hotel with such amenities, a local bathhouse advertised baths for twenty cents.

In later years, Lee Clinton's son, Walton, was to say, "Vinita and Muskogee had two railroads and Sapulpa was closest to the great Glenn Pool oil field, but Tulsa won out because it had more men with nerve and vision than the other towns in those days." Those men (and women) also had the foresight to prohibit drilling for oil within the city's limits, and to plan ahead for schools, hotels, and other facilities to attract those who would be successful in their quest for oil.

Perhaps the prime example of these Tulsans' nerve, however, is the 1905 booster train that carried the young comedian Will Rogers and members of the Commercial Club 2,500 miles across the eastern half of the United States to publicize Tulsa, which at the time had a population near seven thousand. The train carried its own brass band and a printing press to churn out a daily newspaper as they crossed the country. Tate Brady would remember later: "At the time when there was not a man in Tulsa worth more than $15,000, we got 100 Tulsans to lay down $100 each on the barrel head, $10,000 in all— with which we hired a special train and a band to take a load of boosters and exhibits on tour of half of the United States to spread the story and the glory of Tulsa." Among the booster train passengers were Tate Brady, Fred Clinton, Loren Conaway, N.J. Gubser, and Dr. W.M. Wilson.

The booster train was a howling success. Not only did the trip help launch Will Rogers' career, but it generated many pages of newspaper publicity for Tulsa throughout the midwest and east. A Chicago newspaper reported:

> *. . . With a College yell that frightened the echoes, Tulsa's special came in. And this is what the astonished Commercial Club of Chicago learned:*
> *That Tulsa wasn't on the map because it grew faster than maps could be printed.*
> *That Tulsa was a magnificent metropolis of seven churches and not a single saloon.*
> *That the clink of one dollar against another was Tulsa's national air.*

Following the train's arrival in Chicago, the Tulsans visited the Chicago board of trade. Reported the *Chicago Tribune:*

Pandemonium reigned and trade on the exchange stopped for ten minutes today when the Tulsa boosters from Indian Territory, with their band, came on the floor and tore loose on "Dixie." Col. H.H. Brady, a Confederate veteran, gave the rebel yell, while Will Rogers, a Tulsa Indian, did marvelous stunts with a rope. Lee Nichols, editor of the paper that is being published on the train, was asked by a broker, when he said that Tulsa would have a population of 100,000 by 1920, whether Tulsa was in the United States. While the tumult was on, London cabled and inquiring the cause of the cessation of trading was told that the Indian Territory boosters were here.

In the latter half of 1905, some of its members freshly returned from the booster trip, the church took another major step. The brick building at Second and Cincinnati was only three years old, but already it was inadequate for this congregation and their visions for the future. "The board of trustees and official members of the Methodist Episcopal South of Tulsa, I.T., have purchased for a new church location the property known as the John McAlester property on the corner of Boston and Fifth streets, facing south and east, paying six thousand dollars for the same," reported W.L. Britton and J.R. Cole, Jr. "To secure payment [we] have given mortgage on the above described property and on the present church property on the corner of Second and Cincinnati." That property would be sold the following year and the church would be built on a lot diagonally across from the McAlester lot at the same intersection. From this time forward, the church would hold services on Boston Avenue as it had done that first winter of 1893-4 when the founders had met in the old Presbyterian Mission School. The trustees were authorized to sell the present church at Second and Cincinnati as well as the parsonage site for the best price obtainable. W.L. Britton, H.R. Cline, and J.R. Cole, Jr., were elected a building committee to consider all plans necessary for the building of a new church.

At its sixty-first session, in 1906, the Indian Mission Conference of the Methodist Episcopal Church South was officially renamed the "Oklahoma Conference of the Methodist Episcopal Church South."

The Reverend James Henry Ball became Tulsa's new preacher in charge in 1906, and reported that the church had two Sunday schools, with J.R. Cole, Jr., and J.M. Holland as superintendents. "Our Sunday schools are a source of inspiration and pride to us all and much good is being accomplished in them. The general state of the church is very good. Our sabbath congregations just about tax the full capacity of our church."

The Reverend Ball had been licensed to preach in 1888 and ordained a deacon at the Denver Conference in 1893. He came to

Indian Territory in 1905 to preach at Phillips Memorial in Muskogee, later renamed Grand Avenue Church.

In 1906 the Tulsa church's building was overflowing, and the Methodists living north of the railroad tracks began holding Sunday school classes for children and adults at Sequoyah School, with the support of the Reverend Ball. On November 19, 1906, forty-six charter members organized a new Methodist Episcopal Church South to be built north of the tracks. The Reverend Ball persuaded about thirty members to transfer their membership to help build up Tigert Memorial Methodist Church South, which would later be renamed Centenary. When the brick church building at Second and Cincinnati was sold for $17,500 the next year, the conference ordered the church to pay the Tigert Memorial Church $1,500 as their proportionate part of the sale.

Tigert Memorial was named for Bishop John James Tigert who died while in office, two days after the new church was organized. The Reverend Ball, who was pastor at the Tulsa church at the time of the bishop's death, wrote a letter to a Brother Babcock who was working on a history of Methodism saying,

> *These are the facts:*
> *1. A chicken bone lodged in Bishop Tigert's throat at a dinner in Brother Satterfield's home in Lawton.*
> *2. He went from Lawton to Atoka (we don't know how).*
> *3. He came from Atoka to Tulsa by train in the care of Brother W.D. Matthews. I met the train and he was more dead than alive when he got here.*
> *4. His physicians were Dr. Fred Clinton, Dr. J.C.W. Bland, and Bishop Tigert's son who arrived from Nashville a day or two later.*
> *5. He died in Tulsa.*

Notes from the conference minutes in 1906 indicate, "Bishop Tigert opened the conference, but being too ill to preside, Bishop J.S. Key, at his request, presided throughout the session. Bishop Tigert died the day following the adjournment of the conference." A marker later placed at the base of the Brady Hotel noted that he died there.

Tulsa in 1906 had no hospital, and Dr. Clinton often had to perform surgery wherever he could find space. Once, a Deputy U.S. Marshal had been shot twice in the abdomen with a .45, and had seven perforations to his intestines. Dr. Clinton, assisted by Dr. S.G. Kennedy, treated him at the Alcorn Hotel, putting him on a couple of 1' x 12' planks supported by boxes, and operating by gasoline light. The surgery was successful, Dr. Clinton later reported, and the marshal went on to marry and raise a family.

When the American National Red Cross was chartered in 1905, Dr. Clinton had immediately applied for a branch to be located in

Indian Territory. That became a reality in 1906. Later that year Dr. Clinton and several assistants established Tulsa's first hospital, which included a training school for nurses, in a nineteen-room house at Fifth and Lawton that had been a private home. The first extensive street paving had finally begun in Tulsa that year, and the horse drawn ambulance had rubber tires for the comfort of the patients.

Tulsa's first fire station was built in 1906 at 211 West Second Street. It also served as the city hall and the police station. The horses that drew the fire engine were stabled on the first floor, and the jail was in the basement. A yellow brick high school was erected at Fourth and Boston where the Presbyterian Mission School once stood, and steamboat excursions were offered on the Arkansas River. However, one trip down the river for the grand opening of Jenks town site lots took an unexpected turn when the steamboat couldn't get back up the river because of the currents.

Church members Lon and Ida Conaway lived on a homestead that was the south half of the 600 block between Main and Boston. Loren A. Conaway, Jr., born in 1902, was baptized in 1906 and would remain a member of the church for many years.

In December of 1906, a dance card from the Proteus Club filled out by C.C. Cole showed four dances with Miss Rudd. Audrey Lecil Rudd would become Mrs. C.C. Cole in October of 1907 when she was twenty-one and he was twenty-nine. The opposite side of the dance card read:

DR. FRED CLINTON

> *Tulsa Indian Territory has: 2 mills, 1 foundry, 4 hotels, 1 ice plant, 4 elevators,*
> *2 laundries, 1 cotton gin, 1 planing mill, 2 brick plants,*
> *2 bottling works, 5 banks, 2 wholesale houses*
> *25 oil and gas wells*
> *298 residence houses built in past 12 months*
> *14 one-story brick/stone business buildings*
> *47 two-story brick/stone business buildings*
> *$40,000 steel wagon bridge across Arkansas River*
> *3 railroads*
> *Population 1,390 in 1900*
> *3,650 in December 1903.*

By 1907 the church was growing rapidly. The newly-married Mrs. C. C. Cole was one of those who joined the church that year. A Women's Foreign Missionary Society was organized in 1907 at the home of Mrs. Fred Clinton, with the assistance of her sister, Mrs. T.C. Carlton. Mrs. Clinton was elected president, and served in that office until 1915.

On November 16, 1907, came a long-awaited day; Oklahoma became a state. The population in Tulsa was 7,198 up 425 percent in the first seven years of the century. Oklahoma City, Muskogee,

LOREN CONAWAY, JR.

Guthrie and others still were larger. Muskogee, in fact, had more than twice the population of Tulsa, but Tulsa was growing faster. That same year, Kendall College—later to become the University of Tulsa—was moved from Muskogee to Tulsa, and Kendall Hall would open the following year.

There was a building boom on in Tulsa in 1907, with construction underway amounting to half a million dollars. Many of the new business buildings were on Second Street, with construction there amounting to $225,000. Houses were being built as quickly as possible, and 160 were under construction at one time. The average cost for a house was two thousand dollars. It was noted in a local newspaper, "At the present time, it is practically impossible either to rent a business house or a residence. You must apply to rent a building while the foundation is being erected in order to be first on the list."

The church was part of this building boom. In 1907 the cornerstone was laid for an impressive red brick church building with massive columns at Fifth and Boston. Now that there were two ME South congregations in the city, the church could no longer call itself simply "the Methodist Episcopal Church South." The name engraved on the cornerstone was First ME Church South. This, however, caused much confusion, since there was already a First ME Church in town. Thus, when the congregation moved into its new home at Fifth and Boston in March, 1908, the name was changed to Boston Avenue Methodist Episcopal Church South.

The new building had lovely stained glass windows that could be opened in hot weather, a balcony, a center aisle, and classrooms in the basement. It cost forty thousand dollars to build. The Reverend J. H. Ball recalls that at first there was no stove in the basement Sunday

school department, and heat was provided by "lighting the end of a pipe, flambeau style."

J.R. Cole, Jr., a member of the building committee, said, "The real work was done by Brother Ball and W.E. Chastain, one of our members who superintended the construction from start to finish. . . . We were so puffed up with our job and so jealous of our authority that we could take no suggestions from anyone . . . not even the ladies when it came to the interior decorations. The result was that we had a mahogany pulpit and chancel rails with oak pews and communion table."

Miss Mary Davis, the sister of Mrs. W.M. Wilson and Mrs. Tate Brady, donated silver offering plates to the new church.

The church had two hundred members at the time it became "Boston Avenue."

The Church at Fifth & Boston

The Reverend A.F. Smith - 1908-1910
The Reverend J.E. Carpenter - 1910
The Reverend Percy Knickerbocker - 1910-1914

Although early records were sometimes incomplete and often difficult to read, at least they existed. There was a period in the church's history, from 1908 to 1914, about which there are virtually no records to be found. No quarterly records, no files, only a few church listings in the Tulsa newspapers.

Here is what is known.

At the end of August, 1908, J.H. Ball resigned his charge at Boston Avenue Church and the Reverend A.F. Smith from the St. Louis Conference was appointed to take his place. Born in 1869 in Missouri, Smith was educated at Belleview Collegiate Institute, Central College, and Vanderbilt University, gaining honorary A.B., D.D., and Litt.D., degrees. He served Gallaway Memorial Methodist Church in Jackson, Mississippi; St. Pauls and Centenary Churches in St. Louis, Missouri; and was a chaplain at Barnes Hospital in St. Louis. He also edited the *Christian Advocate* of the ME Church South of St. Louis.

A few months after the Reverend Smith's appointment, the church was shown on the records of the annual conference (held November 6 to 11 in Oklahoma City) to have a house of worship valued at $45,000, a total membership of 292, a Sunday school with sixteen officers and teachers and two hundred scholars.

The Reverend Smith served Boston Avenue Church from 1908 until 1910. Little is known about his pastorate in Tulsa, but in March, 1910, he preached on "The Great Inheritance," and on the following evening a meeting was held of all the congregation (the roll of members would be called) on matters pertaining to the enlargement of the work. The presiding elder was to be present, and at the same time would hold the second quarterly conference of the year.

The Easter Sunday service the following week, March 27, was listed in the Tulsa newspaper with the Reverend Smith preaching. There were no further listings until July 3 when an announcement appeared for a Children's Day program at 11:00 a.m., with a short address by Judge L.M. Poe.

The following Sunday, the *Tulsa World* reported that the Reverend J.E. Carpenter from Jackson, Tennessee, had assumed the pastorate of the church. Conference records in November 1910, however, show that he had transferred from the Mississippi Conference where he was an elder.

His sermon at the November conference, preceding the ordination of elders, was apparently an effective one, for the next day a resolution was passed that he be requested to reproduce that sermon in an article for the *Quarterly Review.* About his work in the Tulsa church nothing is known, but a publication in later years praising the sermons of Dr. Grimes said, "His intellectual sermons still shine out with the brilliance of Dr. Carpenter's years ago."

The Reverend Percy Knickerbocker, who read the Epistle at the ordination of deacons and was chairman of the eastern Oklahoma church extension committee at that 1910 conference, was assigned to Tulsa. He had served at St. Luke's church in Oklahoma City from 1907 to 1909, and under his pastorate, that church completed and furnished a building at a cost of $100,000.

A publication of that time wrote, "Reverend Percy Knickerbocker is one of the best known ministers in the state. He is considered to be one of the very best pulpit orators in the Southwest

DR. W. M. WILSON, 1904
DR. WILSON WAS WELL-LOVED THROUGHOUT THE COMMUNITY. HE IS SEEN HERE TAKING SOME FRIENDS FOR A SPIN IN HIS WHITE STANLEY STEAMER.

THE POE HOME
JUDGE AND MRS. L. M. POE RESIDED
AT SEVENTH AND BOSTON.

and all his services are well attended, owing to his wonderful and decidedly original texts."

Walton Clinton, who joined the church in 1908, remembered the Reverend Knickerbocker clearly. He said, "He wore loud checkered suits, raised and sold bird dogs, and liked the horse races."

Several years later, when no membership records could be found, the Reverend Ball, Boston Avenue's former pastor who by this time had become presiding elder of the Tulsa district, helped reconstitute the church roll from his acquaintance, his former pocket record, and help from church members. The Reverend Ball was presiding elder from 1913 until 1917.

Of course, records do exist of what was happening in the city during those years as Tulsa grew rapidly, and Boston Avenue Church members continued to be instrumental in the city's development.

Jane Heard Clinton helped organize the first Parent Teacher Organization in 1908, becoming a charter member of that organization as well as the Ruskin Art Club formed that year. She was the first president of the Ruskin Club.

Vitally interested in helping provide the raw little town with more cultural opportunities, she was active in virtually every organization of that type in town. She was a charter member of the Tulsa Civic Music Association, the Tulsa Garden Club, the Children's Day Nursery, Tulsa Federation of Music Clubs, and a board member of the Tulsa Symphony Orchestra Association. She also served as president of many of those organizations through the years. Her sister-in-law, Susan (Mrs. Lee Clinton), was active in many of the same organizations.

Dr. W.M. Wilson completed his three-floor, yellow-brick office building at 224 East Second in 1908. The *Tulsa World* advertised that July 26, 1908, was the last day to purchase lots in the Gillette-Hall Addition. But few streets were paved by this time, and it was decreed that each man between the ages of eighteen and forty-five would give a full day of work each year to help pave the streets—or pay a three dollar tax.

The *World* also was advertising for carriers. "Need boys with ponies," the ads said. Newspaper subscriptions were ten cents a month, and the *Tulsa World* celebrated its third birthday that year. It had begun as an evening paper, had grown from twelve to thirty-two employees and had a circulation of 5,123.

It was reported that Oklahoma was growing more rapidly than any other state. By 1909, Tulsa had 126 companies or individuals in oil, eighty-four lawyers, eight jewelers, and eleven hotels. Harry Sinclair organized the Exchange National Bank located at Second and Main streets, publicizing it as "a bank run by oil men for oil men." Land for Woodward Park at Twenty-first and Peoria was purchased by the city for one hundred dollars an acre. There was, as happened so often, criticism because it was so far out and "could be reached only by wagon trails."

Tulsa's population in 1909 was nearing fifteen thousand people, seventy-five of whom were teachers. One of those was a young woman named Elsie Heaton, who came to Tulsa that year in spite of her father's fears about the town's bad reputation. She boarded with a Boston Avenue Church member at Fourth and Cheyenne and taught school in the basement of Henry Kendall College for seventy-five dollars a month.

In those days, she would later recall, young single people liked to go to Grandma Parker's Boarding House at Fourth and Cincinnati for dinner. It was there that she met Judge N.J. Gubser, and they were married in 1910.

Judge Gubser was the first Tulsa county judge and had jurisdiction over juvenile offenders. There was no place to keep the juveniles at that time, and he often brought them home. He was instrumental in getting a detention home built near Mohawk Park. The Gubsers were long-time, active members of the church.

In January, it was reported that Oklahoma City was determined to become the state capital in place of Guthrie. The population of Tulsa in 1910 had reached 18,182 and was still growing rapidly. Lillian Russell appeared at the Grand Theater in "The First Night" in February of 1910, and the Robinson Hotel advertised room rates of $2.50 a day and up.

In 1910, the Foreign Missionary Society and the earlier Women's Parsonage and Home Missionary Society merged. The combined group would be known as the Women's Missionary Society.

A runaway gray horse shocked onlookers as it raced down Main Street with a delivery wagon clattering wildly behind it. The lucky driver, who couldn't even slow the horse down, was dumped into a pile of sand by the Brady Hotel and escaped unharmed. The first Boy Scout troop was formed in Tulsa in 1911, and in 1912 the first court house was built at 521 South Boulder.

The home of Judge L.M. Poe and his family was at Seventh and Boston, and one day when the youngest boy, Ned, was two and a half, he and the Judge walked down the street to the church at Fifth and Boston so the little boy could be baptized. He had always been called Ned, but the Judge intended for him to be a lawyer and didn't think that was a dignified enough name for a lawyer. So he had him christened "John Hunter Poe" for a close friend of his. They walked back home, and the Judge announced, "This boy has just been christened. His name is John Hunter Poe and you will call him that." Then, turning to the boy, he said, "Come on, Ned, let's go finish . . ."

At that time Dr. and Mrs. Fred Clinton were living in what was described as a "commodious" house at Fifth and Cheyenne which was noted for its surrounding flower garden. Mrs. Clinton and her fellow members in Hyechka (who re-elected her president every year) continued to work for cultural development during those years when Tulsa was booming. In 1914 they persuaded the city to build a $125,000 convention hall and install a $11,500 organ. Tulsa's Convention Hall (later to be called the Brady Theater) seated 4,200 people and would host the world's foremost performers, speakers, and star attractions through coming generations.

That same year, a new YMCA facility was constructed at Fourth and Cincinnati, boasting the city's first indoor swimming pool. C.C. Cole played an instrumental role, serving on the YMCA's first board of directors. Tulsa's firefighters became fully mechanized in 1914, after selling the last of their horses the year before to Kansas City.

CHAPTER 6

WAR YEARS

DR. LOUIS S. BARTON - 1914-1922
THE REVEREND W.C. HOUSE - 1918-1919

I n 1914 the Reverend Knickerbocker was transferred to the North Texas Conference, and Dr. Louis S. Barton began an eight-year term as pastor of Boston Avenue Methodist Episcopal Church South.

Louis Samuel Barton entered the ministry in 1893 in the North Texas Conference, and had served churches in Texas since that time. His courtship of his wife Jane, as related later by Grace McCrary, had captured the imagination of his congregation. A Texas girl, she was studying Bible in Nashville, Tennessee, with the intention of becoming a Bible teacher. At one point when Dr. Barton's suit was insistent, she said, "But I can't marry you because I've promised God I would teach Bible." He replied, "Well, I'm not exactly the devil. Marry me and I'll still let you teach Bible." She did, of course, and they moved to Tulsa in 1914, living in the parsonage at 817 South Boston.

Far more formal in demeanor than his predecessor at Boston Avenue Church, Barton entered the pulpit each Sunday wearing a cutaway morning coat, striped trousers and a stiff collar. Members of

OLD, OLD CENTRAL HIGH SCHOOL
GRACE MCCRARY, IN WHITE, AND OTHER STUDENTS DURING THE LAST YEAR AT THE "OLD, OLD CENTRAL HIGH SCHOOL" IN 1917.

THE BREWER HOME

TAKEN IN 1917, THIS PHOTOGRAPH FEATURES THE HOME OF DR. AND MRS. F. L. BREWER AT THIRTEENTH AND TROOST. STANDING ON THE PORCH ARE THE FAMILY OF DONNA BREWER BYNUM AND THE GRANDDAUGHTERS OF DR. AND MRS. BREWER.

the congregation recall Dr. Barton's powerful preaching, his pastoral care, and especially his affection for and popularity with young people. It was later said of him that his work was characterized by saintliness, devotion, sound scholarship, and evangelical conviction.

In later years, J.P. Byrd III, who was baptized by Dr. Barton in 1916 or early 1917, remembers going to the home of the Lee Clintons, to whom he was related. "I was only three or four years old, and sometimes Dr. Barton was there. I'm sure he was gentle and kindly, but his booming, 'foghorn' voice was a little frightening."

Dr. Barton's long tenure at Boston Avenue would be prove to be a boon to the church. It was under his guidance that the congregation outgrew the church building at Fifth and Boston.

One project for which Dr. Barton worked diligently was to establish a Methodist university in Tulsa. In this he was supported by Bishop Edwin Mouzon, but was unsuccessful. He then gave strong support to Oklahoma City University and served as a vice-president of that institution.

Charles and Anna Crotchett moved to Tulsa in 1917 with their three daughters, Anne K., Ruth, and Mary Jane, so that Mr. Crotchett could open a branch office for his brokerage firm. Anne would later recall her first impressions of the town after Mr. Crotchett met them at the train station at Second and Main. Not all the streets were paved and there were no sidewalks, just narrow paths beaten through the tall weeds. A streetcar ran from downtown to Eighteenth Street along Main. Most homes still had a hitching post in front, but Tulsa's favorite mode of transportation—both public and private—was rapidly becoming the automobile. Cars with signs on them saying "Jitney" would stop for people on corners and take them downtown for ten cents. If you had a family car, Anne Crotchett would later recall, you almost always took a drive on Sunday afternoon.

During the late teens the Model T virtually replaced the horse and buggy on the streets of Tulsa. With the popularity of the automobile, demand for oil grew rapidly, and the city boomed. Central High School on Sixth Street between Cincinnati and Detroit was completed in 1916. Its student population grew so fast that an additional wing had to be built on the south just five years later. A two-lane bridge across the Arkansas River replaced the 1903 toll bridge at Eleventh Street. (It would be widened in 1935 to four lanes, forming a link in the Route 66 highway which crossed the nation.)

Buildings and houses were scarce in the fast-developing young city, yet people continued to arrive. So many freight cars were tied up with furniture in the Tulsa freight yards that the Frisco and Santa Fe refused to receive any cargo that did not have an address where it could be delivered. Mr. Crotchett rented office space on the front balcony of a Chinese restaurant across from the Tulsa Hotel on Third Street.

The Women's Christian Temperance Union was born in Tulsa in February 1917, at the home of Lilah D. Lindsey. Fifty women attended that first meeting; one arrived in a surrey with fringe and another rode sidesaddle. The WCTU raised four hundred dollars that day, and borrowed one hundred dollars from one member to pay down on property at 719 South Quincy for the Frances Willard Home for Girls. They took the five hundred dollars in pennies, nickels, and dollar bills to make the down payment on the $6,500 cost. They would later sell that property and subsequent ones, ultimately buying forty acres in the Osage Hills just northwest of town which became the permanent site of the home. After paying off the Osage Hills property, the WCTU turned the Frances Willard Home over to the Oklahoma Methodist Conference.

The United States entered the World War in 1917, and the Tulsa Ambulance Company packed up and went to France to join the famed Rainbow Division. Almost the entire Kendall College football team belonged to the Ambulance Company. Oil refineries in Tulsa increased their output twenty-five percent for the war effort.

The Marine Corps recruiting station was next door to the headquarters of the Tulsa County Council of Defense on Main Street. The Council, which coordinated all civilian defense efforts, offered fifty dollars for every draft dodger rounded up. It sponsored patriotic

NELLIE CLULOW

community sings, the "Victory Chorus," which sometimes drew as many as twenty thousand Tulsans. The Red Cross Canteen, which served thousands of service men passing through, was near the Frisco Depot.

Dr. Barton took a year's leave of absence in 1918-1919 to serve as a chaplain to American soldiers in the European army of occupation through the YMCA Chaplaincy Service. In his place the YMCA sent the Reverend W.C. House to serve as Boston Avenue Church's interim minister.

Tuberculosis was the number one killer in the United States, and Tulsa's Public Health Association was formed in 1918 to fight it. In 1919, Bob Bradshaw came to Tulsa, and he would become a vital member of the congregation in years to come. L.C. Clark and Sybil Brown were married that year, and Mrs. Ernest E. (Nellie Cornelia) Clulow became the church organist, a post she would hold until her death in 1939. She was active in Hyechka and many music associations.

When the war was over, Tulsans spent $3,500 to erect a replica of the Arc de Triomphe which they called the Arch of Welcome, to welcome returning service men and women. Tulsa continued to boom, and Boston Avenue Church members continued to play prominent roles in their city's growth.

In 1920, Walton Clinton was instrumental in establishing the Tulsa Jaycees. The population of Tulsa reached 72,075 in the 1920 census, vastly outdistancing the once-larger Muskogee, whose

FRIENDS REUNITED

MRS. K.Y. TUTTLE, C.C. MCCRARY, GRACE TUTTLE, AND KATHRYN YEAGER. MCCRARY WAS ON LEAVE DURING A TOUR OF DUTY AT FORT LOGAN IN HOUSTON, TEXAS.

population then was only 30,277. Kendall College, which had moved from Muskogee thirteen years before, became the University of Tulsa.

That year also saw the birth of the Married Folks class, the first in the church that married couples could attend together. C.J. Allen, an assistant to Dr. Barton, had heard of classes for young marrieds elsewhere. He talked to Dr. Barton and to Carl Duffield, Sunday school superintendent. Duffield was given the task of organizing and guiding the new class. By the end of that first year, the class included forty-six married couples and one single person. Matt S. Webster was the first president, and he was to remain a loyal and faithful member of the class for more than fifty years. During those fifty years, Mrs. Alva Fry was the only lady elected president of the class. Judge Henry Fulling was the first teacher.

Another member of the legal profession would become a favorite teacher. Alex Johnston, a lawyer, was so compelling that class members talked about him years later in glowing terms. Especially memorable was his verbal depiction of Christ's trial from a legal standpoint. With Johnston as teacher, the Married Folks class eventually grew to some twelve hundred members, "the largest in the United States," according to long-time member Kathryn Menard. It was "wonderful," Eunice Mauzy recalled. "It was organized in groups

THE WAR YEARS
ABOVE LEFT, CHURCH MEMBERS HOLD THE WORLD WAR I BOSTON AVENUE SERVICE FLAG. DIRECTLY ABOVE ARE CARL C. MCCRARY (TOP) AND VIRGIL RADER (BELOW).

MORE
THAN A
BUILDING

of twenty-five, and we looked after our own."

J. Earl Simpson joined the church in 1921 and soon volunteered to be an usher. At the time he had no idea that he would continue to usher at Boston Avenue for the next fifty-eight years.

Another new member in 1921 was Natalie [Mrs. W.K.] Warren, who joined the church on October 31. The month before she had married W.K. Warren, who had come to Tulsa from Nashville in 1916 to work for Gypsy Oil. In 1922 Mr. Warren would start his own oil company, Warren Petroleum. During the next seventy-two years, Mrs. Warren would remain a loyal member, supporting her church with many generous gifts. The Warrens had seven children, and founded Saint Francis Hospital, which was completed in 1960.

The Young Matrons' Missionary Society was organized in 1921 when Mrs. L.S. Barton and Mrs. L.B. Dawes invited a group of young women that they thought would be interested. Mrs. Barton is remembered by Elizabeth Wilson Smith as "Lovely. The epitome of a southern gentlewoman." She fit the description Bishop W. Angie Smith was fond of tagging on the wives of Methodist ministers— "Queens of the Parsonage."

The women who formed the first panel of officers of the Young Matrons' Missionary Society were names that would go down in the history of the church for their many contributions and hard work. Mrs. A.C. Hunt was elected president and Mrs. C.C. McCrary, vice president. Other officers included Mrs. L. Weist, Mrs. O.S. Landrith, Mrs. J.J. Jackson, Mrs. Russell Lee, Mrs. M.H. Watts, Mrs. H.R. Robinson and Mrs. L.S. Barton. The next year a publication called *Tulsa's Churches* reported, ". . . all the Women's Societies of the church united and are now known as The Missionary Society. They are doing a wonderful good."

In 1921, the J.M. Gillettes built the large English Tudor mansion at Fifteenth and Yorktown as a country retreat. The arched bridge across the Arkansas River at Twenty-first Street was begun that same year. Other, less happy events were to take place that year, when racial tension erupted into a race riot that would leave scars on the community and its people for many years to come.

In 1922, Dr. Barton was assigned to the Methodist Episcopal Church South in Norman where the McFarlin Memorial Methodist Church was built during the five years he was minister there. He later served St. Paul Methodist Church in Muskogee while construction was underway there.

He returned to Tulsa in 1927 as presiding elder (P.E.), a position that would later be called district superintendent. He was much in demand as a preacher, and preached somewhere almost every Sunday, but Mrs. Barton put her membership in at Boston Avenue.

They established a home at 1350 East 19th Street, where one of Dr. Barton's favorite pieces of furniture was a large rocking chair with a tall back that had once belonged to the famed singer John MacCormack. "It just fit him," Mrs. Barton said. He also found time in his schedule for some hunting with Carl Duffield, and to work on the Bartons' farm near Tulsa where he enjoyed planting, grafting, and

**THE YOUNG MATRONS'
MISSIONARY SOCIETY**
DR. AND MRS. BARTON ARE
PICTURED WITH MEMBERS OF THE
SOCIETY IN 1922.

developing pecans. His doctorate was bestowed by Southern Methodist University in 1930.

Dr. Barton retired in 1940 after forty-seven years as an active Methodist minister. During his career, he represented his church at three general conferences, was a delegate to the Ecumenical Conference at London, the Conference of Life and Work at Stockholm—and ten years later at Oxford, and the Conference of Faith and Order at Edinburgh, Scotland.

One day in 1953, while Dr. Barton was gone bird hunting, Bishop Galloway called Mrs. Barton and asked if he could come by and see her. He recalled that when he arrived, she was beautifully groomed and perfectly poised. She said, "You have come to tell me about Louis." She had been concerned about his not being well enough to go bird hunting, and correctly sensed that his death had occurred.

Dr. Barton's name will live forever at Boston Avenue Church through the Barton Lectureship Foundation established in his memory in 1962 by Mrs. Barton and her son Lee. Their goal was to secure the world's best speakers in the philosophy of religion, and the annual lectures would be open to the public. The first speaker selection committee was Mrs. Barton, Lee Barton, Dr. Finis Crutchfield, Dr. Hugh Perry, then Boston Avenue board chairman, and Dr. Ira E. Williams, the area superintendent for the Methodist Church.

Always known as a scholar and a powerful preacher, Dr. Barton was one of Methodism's best educated men. The foundation is a fitting tribute to the man who was so loved and revered in Tulsa.

Mrs. Barton also instituted the church's missionary endowment fund and contributed generously to it, helping assist the church's medical workers in Bolivia.

CHAPTER 7

GROUNDBREAKING

DR. JOHN A. RICE - 1922-1927

r. John A. Rice, a South Carolina native, came to Boston Avenue Church in 1922 at the age of sixty. He was destined to be the guiding force in one of the most significant developments in the history of the church, the Thirteenth and Boston Building.

After his graduation from Old South Carolina College, John Rice had married a minister's daughter, Anna Belle Smith, and they had three children, John Andrew, Liston McLeod, and Coke Smith, before Mrs. Rice's death in 1899. Rice served as a minister in the South Carolina Conference in 1886, then as president of Columbia College.

The year after his wife's death, Rice resigned to work on his Ph.D. at the University of Chicago. While there, he met and married another student, Launa Darnell. After finishing his class work at Chicago, he served as a minister in several states. During these years, he and Launa had two children, Richard Darnell and Elizabeth.

In 1920 he assumed the position as head of the Old Testament History Department at Southern Methodist University in Texas. A book which he published, *The Old Testament in the Life of Today,* proved to be unexpectedly controversial and he resigned to spare the university embarrassment.

Dr. Rice must have been a convincing preacher in the pulpit, because Hughie Pressley Williamson, a secretary, sat between the pulpit and the altar rail each Sunday morning, typing his sermons on a silent stenotype machine as he delivered them. She then mimeographed copies to sell to members at ten cents apiece to defray the costs of the machine. "We always sold at least three hundred, and usually five hundred at Christmas and Easter. Visitors as well as church members wanted them," she said. C.C. Cole, who had by now been a leading layman at the church for two decades, had his own standards for sermons preached from the Boston Avenue pulpit. He timed them, and the short ones were proclaimed "good."

In 1922 Mr. and Mrs. C.C. Cole became the proud parents of their third daughter, Elizabeth Deane, and built a spacious home which they named "Rockmoor" on East Twenty-second Street, where the Jaycee headquarters would one day stand. Mary Caroline (Tot) Cole

C. C. COLE

THE COLES
AUDREY COLE WITH MARY
CAROLINE, AUDREY, AND ELIZABETH.

had been born in 1912, and Audrey Lee in 1917. The Cole's friends, the Harwells, built a thirty-room home they called "Harwelden" across the street the following year. It would one day be the home of the Arts and Humanities Council of Tulsa. Mrs. Cole helped establish the Shakespeare Club during that same busy year. When the International Petroleum Exposition was organized by W.G. Skelly in 1923, the chairman of the social committee for the first two of the great oil shows to be held in Tulsa was another well-known Boston Avenue Church lady, Jane Heard Clinton. First held at Convention Hall, the IPE would become one of the world's largest trade shows.

Mrs. Rice, the pastor's wife, was often called the "city's number one mother." Left motherless herself at the age of eight, she had mothered her two younger sisters, and then her husband's children when she married Dr. Rice. She lost her first son at age fifteen months, and said later she felt that might not have happened had she known more about child care. She earned a degree from the Nashville College of Women and later an advanced degree from the University of Chicago and a masters from Columbia University. A home counselor in the Tulsa school system, she was very concerned about parents helping their children grow up mentally and physically healthy. In 1923 she established the Mothers Club, for the two-fold purpose of "lending all available help toward the right training of children in the home, and of bringing into the foreground of community thinking the place and importance of the child." Under the presidency of Launa Rice, the little club which began with eleven members grew into city-wide importance.

J. Earl Simpson organized the first Boy Scout troop at Boston Avenue in 1922. Troop 20 began with two Cub Scout packs and was destined to become the largest troop in Oklahoma. This would be a strong influence on the lives of boys growing up in Boston Avenue

Church for many years, and at the time of the church's centennial seventy-one years later was the oldest Boy Scout troop in Tulsa.

A terrible flood devastated West Tulsa in 1923. The railroad bridge across the Arkansas River was threatened by the rising water, and as a last resort, a train was parked on the bridge for weight to keep it from washing away.

Anne Crotchett would later report that during the early 1920s, the railroad often blocked Main Street with freight cars. Tulsa continued to boom, and available houses were so scarce many people bought lots and built garages on them to live in until their houses were completed. Then, when they moved into the house, they often rented the garage to a black couple in exchange for domestic help three or four days a week.

One of the factors which had long hampered Tulsa's growth was the lack of good drinking water. Arkansas River water was too salty to be palatable. Early-day springs had been located where Horace Mann School was later built at Tenth and Boston, and the Indians had used springs at Fourteenth and Galveston and on Seventeenth between Cheyenne and the river. In 1906 Dr. S.G.

THE FIFTH AND BOSTON BUILDING
AS SEEN IN THIS PICTURE, THE CHURCH AT FIFTH AND BOSTON WAS DWARFED BY NEWER DOWNTOWN BUILDINGS.

Kennedy and Mark Carr had formed a business to sell and distribute drinking water from Osage Spring. Later entrepreneurs brought in bottled water from various other places, but the favorite was water from Spavinaw, sixty miles east of Tulsa.

In 1924 Tulsa finally got a decent water supply when Spavinaw water was brought in by pipeline. City Water Commissioner, A.J. Rudd, father of Audrey (Mrs. C.C.) Cole, was given much of the credit for this accomplishment. Voters had approved $7.5 million to fund the daring engineering plan to bring water the sixty-mile distance from Spavinaw Lake by gravity flow. When a lake was built to store the water north of Tulsa, Mohawk Park was created.

Voters were generous in 1924, and also approved $3.5 million for a Union Depot. Telephones were being installed in Tulsa at the rate of 260 a month in 1925, C.C. Cole reported in a letter to Audrey, who was out of town for a few weeks.

Not surprisingly, the church at Fifth and Boston was having growing pains. The building which had seemed so spacious in 1906 was beginning to feel like a too-tight pair of shoes. The Married Folks class outgrew its space, and the members bought lumber and built their own classroom on a lot adjoining the church. Sunday school classes were meeting in Central High School, the Orpheum Theater, and the new YMCA building at Fifth and Cheyenne.

The church paid the YMCA six dollars each Sunday for the use of rooms for the Sunday school, and in May of 1927, the electric bill for the church was $12.21, water was $1.40, and the telephone bill totalled $9.29. A broom was purchased from Vandevers Department Store for $1.25. Salaries in the music department included one hundred dollars monthly for Belle Vickery Matthews, seventy-five dollars for Mrs. E.E. Clulow, and lesser amounts for Miss Nettie Huggins, W.D. Thomas and Edward Eitelman.

Church expenses would never again be so modest. In 1924, Dr. Rice appointed a building committee headed by C.C. Cole to plan construction of a new church building. The committee met for the first time on June 9 at the home of Mrs. J.M. Gillette at Fifteenth and Yorktown.

J.R. Cole, Jr., was appointed chairman of the building finance committee, and immediately began the work of raising the necessary funds. The church's congregation at this time numbered less than fourteen hundred, and there were eventually six hundred subscribers to the building fund.

Anne Crotchett described the efforts of some church members toward the new building in a paper entitled "Who's That in the Kitchen?":

While the new church was being built, the Women's Missionary Society prepared and served dinners at the Fifth and Boston church to earn money for their $10,000 pledge.

Dinners were priced at 50 cents and often were chicken a la king, prepared in the too-small church kitchen (after the women cooked the chickens at home and brought in the meat and broth). Green beans were inexpensive at the Trenton Market, and Mrs. Theodore Cox insisted on cooking them the southern way, in butter...instead of that cheaper white oleomargarine."

Grace Tuttle (later to be Mrs. C. C. McCrary), a student at Central High School, often peeled potatoes after school while her mother, Mrs. Kate Tuttle made the butterhorn rolls (for which the Boston Avenue cooks became famous.) The Tuttles lived on Eighteenth Street near the end of the Main Street streetcar line.

A quiet ceremony in the church parsonage drew a great deal of attention in 1925. Dr. W.M. Wilson, at age fifty-eight, was married to seventeen-year old Elizabeth Baer. The pioneering dentist and civic leader had by now been a church stalwart for twenty-three years; he had been widowed for fifteen years. The couple had met when he bought the Baer family plantation in Louisiana, and Elizabeth and her mother subsequently moved to Tulsa and lived in the Wilson Apartments. The marriage would last thirty-five years, ending only in Dr. Wilson's death at the age of ninety-two.

The Mayo Hotel was completed in 1925, and dinner there cost $1.50. In 1926, eighteen-year-old Norma Smallwood, who lived with her mother at the Wilson Apartments and was a friend of Mrs. W.M. Wilson, was named Miss America. She was outfitted for the contest by Vandevers. That year another booster train, called the Tulsa Education Special, rolled off to tell the eastern cities of the United States about the virtues of Tulsa, Oklahoma. A skyline of the city was painted on the side of the train. Inside, the train carried a miniature working refinery and a printing press to print a daily newspaper, along with more than a hundred Tulsa businessmen—many of them Boston Avenue members.

While the building committee sifted through proposed designs and the finance committee began to seek pledges, the work of the church never faltered. In 1926, the church was involved in home missions, an Indian mission and school for Indian youths, schools for immigrant Mexican boys and girls in Texas, work with soldiers and sailors, city and industrial projects, and help for "colored" schools and rural projects.

Bruce Norman joined the church that year, to begin more than sixty years of service as an usher. "I can't sing, they won't let me preach, so how else can I serve my church?" he said.

Mrs. W.H. Mayo, who had visited other churches as a bride

THE WILSON FAMILY
DR. W. M. WILSON
WITH HIS WIFE AND
DAUGHTER, BOTH NAMED
ELIZABETH, IN 1936.

and felt like a stranger, felt welcomed when she and her husband visited Boston Avenue. They joined, vowing that it would never be a cold and unfeeling church. They did their part, greeting people in the aisles each Sunday, organizing greeters, and convincing church circles to assume responsibility for supplying greeters for Sunday morning.

Mrs. Belle Vickery Matthews, director of music, was granted a leave of absence to make a short concert tour. Mrs. Field took her place as soloist and Mrs. E.E. Clulow directed the choir. Church ball teams battled one another and the Fathers and the Mothers clubs planned a joint picnic. W.D. Thomas was put in charge of securing 150 Bibles for the children of West Tulsa who had none. The Sunday school had 918 pupils enrolled, with sixty-eight teachers and officers. L.F. Sensabaugh was director of religious education, Dr. P.P. Claxton was superintendent of Sunday schools, and Mrs. J.R. Cole, Jr., was president of the Women's Missionary Society.

Miss Adah Robinson, head of the art department at the University of Tulsa, conducted a lecture series at the church on church architecture in 1926. Miss Robinson helped Elizabeth Rice, just graduated from Randolph Macon Woman's College, get a job in the advertising department of Brown-Dunkin Department Store. Elizabeth used her artistic talent and training drawing illustrations for the ads.

By this time, plans for the new church building, designed by Adah Robinson, were well underway. A lot had been purchased at Eighth and Boston some time before Dr. Rice came to Boston Avenue, but he and several members of the building committee had their eyes on another site at Thirteenth and Boston. A beautiful church building here, where the avenue curved, would dominate the view as one

moved south out of downtown along Boston. They eventually prevailed; the Thirteenth Street lot was purchased and the Eighth Street lot sold. A large apartment house, seven homes and six stores on the property were moved or demolished.

Groundbreaking for the new church took place on May, 16, 1927—a cloudy, drizzly day that couldn't dampen the enthusiasm of those gathered for the festivities. Dr. John Rice presided and Dr. Fred Clinton outlined the church's history. The first spadeful of dirt was turned by Mrs. Vinnie J. Campbell, an employee in the shoe department of Kahn Mercantile Company. She had earned the honor by making the initial contribution toward the new building long before church officials had definitely decided to build. Dr. F.L. Brewer and his daughter, Lola Brewer Hunt, pioneer members of the church, traveled more than five hundred miles to take part in the ceremonies.

CHAPTER 8

PLANNING THE CHURCH

What an unusual committee Dr. Rice had appointed! Building committees, particularly church building committees, usually are extremely conservative. Almost inevitably they make the safe choice of traditional architecture. But this committee was made up of strong individuals with vision and courage. Their vision was immediately apparent, and their courage was displayed when they stuck to their convictions no matter what.

Chaired by C.C. Cole, the committee consisted of J.R. Cole, Jr., H.G. Barnard, C.E. Duffield, Virgil P. Rader, Mrs. Kate Hagler, Mrs. J.M. Gillette, C.P. Yadon, R.P. Brewer, Lon Stansbery, Dr. F.S. Clinton (serving on his third building committee for the church), and Mrs. F.P. Walter.

MISS ADAH ROBINSON

It was Mrs. Roy Lundy who had first visualized the site at Thirteenth and Boston as ideal for the church. A prominent Tulsan, J.J. McGraw, commented after the church was finished,"Who in your membership had the vision to pick that spot for your church? It is a commanding site. As you drive toward it down Boston Avenue, the church overpowers you. My God, you can't get away from it!"

Dr. Rice had some very clear ideas about what the building should be and do. He repeatedly said, "We must have a creation, not just a building. I'm not sure I'll know one when I see it on paper, but we must be assured we have it before we begin." He also said he wanted "a church before which he could stand in the rain and let it talk to him, and with an interior that would impel him to worship whether he wanted to or not."

He and Mrs. Rice had toured Europe, visiting churches and cathedrals, and came home convinced that a traditional style of architecture was not what Boston Avenue

THE BUILDING COMMITTEE

C. P. YADON

H. G. BARNARD

V. P. RADER

MRS. F. P. WALTER

C. C. COLE, CHAIRMAN

MRS. J. M. GILLETTE

J. R. COLE, JR.

MRS. J. D. HAGLER

L. R. STANSBERY

C. E. DUFFIELD

DR. F. S. CLINTON

R. P. BREWER

Church needed. Mr. and Mrs. C.C. Cole, meanwhile, were visiting churches throughout this country.

The committee talked to architects, most of whom suggested some period style, such as gothic or classic or colonial. One firm submitted several sketches and the committee signed a hasty contract with them. When their more complete ideas were submitted, they included several different tower options which could be used with the main building. Mrs. Cole and several others felt strongly that the tower was essential but that it should be an integral part of the design and not an interchangeable part. After much discussion and impassioned pleas on the part of Mrs. Cole, the firm was dismissed and paid off.

In the booklet "A Twentieth Century Church," published at the time of the building's dedication, Audrey Cole (who modestly refers to herself throughout the book as "C.W." — Chairman's Wife) writes: "The chairman then said to C.W., 'now you've been active in your objections to our plans. Why don't you show us something you think is good?'"

She knew Miss Adah Robinson through some of the art organizations of which she was a member, and valued her opinion. So she went to her and told her of the problem. She asked if Miss Robinson could help, and was told she could try.

A few days later, Miss Robinson went to the Cole home with a sketch rolled up in her hand. She told Mr. and Mrs. Cole to "prepare for a shock," but they weren't really prepared for the stunningly different design she unrolled before them. The vertical lines and round auditorium were significant departures from anything they had seen before.

They telephoned Dr. Rice, who arrived quickly. "One look from him and the architectural boat had struck the Rock of Gibraltar," related Audrey Cole. "Right now, I lock horns with you," he said. He particularly was opposed to the round auditorium. At least he was at first. "By that time, however, the plan had begun to grip the chairman as things fundamentally right are apt to do. His comment to Miss Robinson and to Audrey Cole was 'you've sold it to me. Now sell it to the rest of the committee.' Ground was gained slowly at first. A number of meetings and several dinners were required to arouse the desired enthusiasm, but in the end all succumbed to the spell of the new idea. In a short time Dr. Rice became one of the greatest enthusiasts and helped to win over the doubting Thomases," Audrey Cole related.

Even before they began to discuss who would build the building, they were arguing over brick versus stone. Mr. Barnard, Dr. Rice and several others held out for stone, even though it was more expensive, and they finally prevailed. "Everyone is happy now over

COREOPSIS

ADAH ROBINSON'S INTERPRETATION OF THE COREOPSIS FLOWER, SEEN IN HER SKETCH ABOVE, WAS INCORPORATED THROUGHOUT THE CHURCH — IN PLASTER, WOOD, METAL, AND GLASS.

the final choice. The brown shades in the stone blend beautifully with the terra cotta figures which adorn it," Audrey Cole related later. "The tower, though glorious, was expensive, but it was allowed to remain when the chairman refused to give it up. At one time when the finances were being weighed carefully and despondently, someone proposed that only the tower be built and that of stone. The remark caused much laughter and the tension was broken. This debate, however, continued for several months."

One concession to the budget was made when it was decided that the tower interior would not be completed with the rest of the construction but would wait until a need for the space developed.

In January 1926, it was announced in the church newspaper that the revised plans for the new church were in and could be viewed in the office of C.C. Cole. In his campaign report, J.R. Cole, Jr., reported that $325,000 had been pledged, the old parsonage and old church would bring $300,000, leaving $100,000 to be raised.

In May of that year, the paper contained a report from C.C. Cole. "The building committee has been very busy studying and developing plans and very shortly will have something to show the church. We believe that now is the time to go slowly and not make any mistakes. After the plans are finally adopted and fully perfected, there will be no occasion for further delay and we will go forward with a full head of steam."

Audrey Cole wrote, "The next problem was to employ the

TRITOMA — FROM A FLOWER TO A BANNISTER
THE TRITOMA SYMBOL BECAME A FAVORITE FEATURE OF THE BUILDING.

C.C. COLE'S OFFICE

DURING CONSTRUCTION OF THE THIRTEENTH AND BOSTON BUILIDNG, C. C. COLE'S OFFICE WAS A MAIN MEETING PLACE FOR THE BUILDING COMMITTEE.

THE BOSTON AVENUE CHURCH TOWER, 1927

EVEN THE STEEL STRUCTURE OF THE CHURCH'S TOWER WAS IMPRESSIVE TO THOSE DRIVING SOUTH ON BOSTON AVENUE.

architects. Since Miss Robinson was not an engineer, she interviewed the firm of Rush, Endacott and Rush, and reported that she believed they could carry on the work in conjunction with her. Their record was investigated and found satisfactory. To be sure they had never built a church like this, but who had? In the triangular arrangement the committee signed a contract for Miss Robinson to supervise all the art features. That sounded simple enough to her and to the committee. Now they know it meant labor and pain. Indeed the committee soon awoke to the fact that the art features were involved in every inch of the way, from the top of the tower down to the tiniest piece of hardware."

Miss Robinson was an artist, not an architect, as Audrey Cole points out. (Oklahoma was not to have a female architect until after 1945 when the Coles' daughter Mary Caroline became the first). Discussions had been held with several architects, but most were reluctant to tackle such a "radical" building.

The main reason Miss Robinson suggested Rush, Endacott and Rush, a local architectural firm, was that Bruce Goff, a twenty-two-year-old former art student of hers, was a draftsman for them. She felt that he was someone she could work with in carrying out the concepts and designs she had formulated. Rush, Endacott and Rush

assured the committee that they would be glad to work with Miss
Robinson and use her suggestions and ideas.

Early records indicate clearly the concept and original design
were Adah Robinson's, and that Bruce Goff was an essential part of the
firm that took those concepts and designs and developed architectural
plans from which the building was constructed. From concept to
design, to architectural plan, to actual construction, all the different
stages required great talent, and each was essential to the other. A
unique and stunningly beautiful "modern cathedral" was the result of

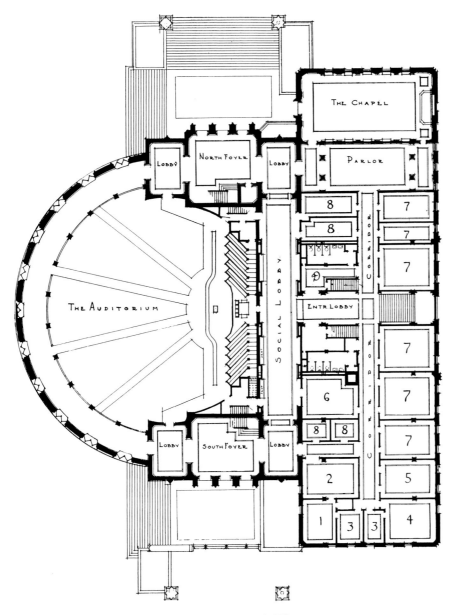

Second Floor

1. PASTOR'S STUDY
2. Reception Room
3. OFFICES
4. LIBRARY
5. RELIGIOUS DIRECTOR
6. S. S. LITERATURE ROOM
7. YOUNG PEOPLES CLASS ROOMS
8. COAT ROOMS
9. KITCHENETTE

  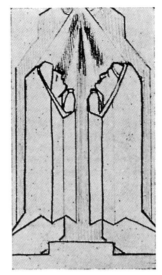 

PRAYERS IN WOOD AND STONE

ABOVE ARE ADAH ROBINSON'S SKETCHES FOR CARVINGS ON THE SANCTUARY COMMUNION TABLE. RIGHT: ONE OF THE MOST POPULAR AND FAMILIAR FEATURES OF THE CHURCH ARE ITS SIXTY-TWO PRAYING HANDS. ADAH ROBINSON NOTED THAT "CLOSED LINES AND HORIZONTAL LINES HAVE BEEN ASSOCIATED WITH FINALITY. MODERN LINES ARE FLOWING, UPWARD, OPEN, FREE. THESE MODERN HANDS, OPEN, ARE CONFIDENT OF THE RECEPTIVITY OF DIVINE GRACE."

BOSTON AVENUE
UNITED METHODIST
CHURCH

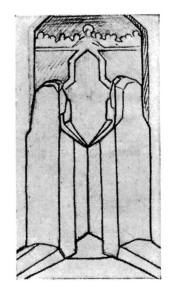 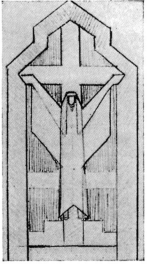 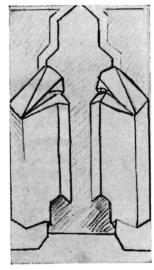 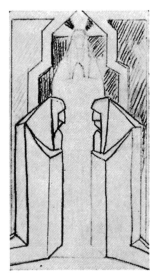

this inspired work.

The contracts signed with Miss Robinson and with Rush, Endacott and Rush on June 26, 1926, specify that Adah Robinson was to be in charge of all things artistic, both inside and outside the building, and for carrying out the wishes of the church. For her work she was to receive five thousand dollars (which was later doubled because there was so much more work involved than was originally envisioned). Rush, Endacott and Rush were contracted to "furnish preliminary sketches, contract and working drawings, detail drawings and specifications, and general supervision of the building operations." The architects would receive five percent of the cost of the building, not to exceed twenty-five thousand dollars.

Adah Robinson was a Quaker and knew little about Methodism. She spent the entire first summer researching Methodist history, and developed symbolism for the church that is as significant today as it was then. When she was through, every line, every sculpture, every window, and every detail expressed a thought. "The church was designed artistically to honor God, to serve as an inspiration for the ages, and to identify its members as people of God," she said.

There are dozens of stories about the development and construction of the church. A favorite tale is that while the church was still on paper, Mr. Cole picked up the plans and swung them around so that the auditorium faced west as it does now, instead of facing north as was originally planned. He was determined that the tower be in the center of Boston Avenue. Jean Hagler Pinkerton, whose mother was on the building committee, would remember years later that Dr. Rice insisted there be no center aisle in sanctuary. "'I won't preach to an empty aisle,' he said." Miss Robinson kept a drawing board beside her bed throughout the construction of the church, lest an idea escape.

There would eventually be so much strife between the

Charles Wesley · William McKendree · Francis Asbury · William Coppers

THE CIRCUIIT RIDERS

ABOVE ARE DRAWINGS MADE BY ADAH ROBINSON AS SHE ENVISIONED THE FIGURES OVER THE DOORS OF THE BUILDING TO BE SCULPTED IN TERRA COTTA. ON THE FACING PAGE ARE THE FINISHED SCULPTURES OF THE CIRCUIT RIDERS JUST BEFORE THEY WERE SENT TO TULSA TO BE PLACED OVER THE SOUTH ENTRANCE TO THE CHURCH. THESE HONOR THE EARLY PASTORS WHO DID SO MUCH TO SPREAD METHODISM THROUGHOUT THE NEW COUNTRY. ON THE RIGHT IS FRANCIS ASBURY, FATHER OF AMERICAN METHODISM. ON THE LEFT IS WILLIAM MCKENDRIE, THE FIRST AMERICAN-BORN BISHOP. IN THE CENTER IS THE UNKNOWN CIRCUIT RIDER, WHO HONORS ALL THOSE WHO SERVED. FIGURES REPRESENTING SPIRITUAL UPLIFT, BROTHERLY LOVE, AND HUMAN SERVICE ARE BELOW THE CIRCUIT RIDERS. A BIBLICAL INSCRIPTION IS CARVED ON THE LINTEL.

architects and Miss Robinson that meetings had to be held in the offices of C.C. Cole. "C.W. [Audrey Cole], during the long period of stress, would point her finger at Miss Robinson daily and say 'But you're a woman.' That seemed to give 'the woman' fresh courage to contend for principles through the various crises which continued to occur," Audrey Cole related.

Another of Miss Robinson's gifted pupils, Robert Garrison, had become a well-known sculptor in New York. He was commissioned to carry out themes and basic designs created by Miss Robinson for the various sculptured figures that would adorn the church.

Dr. Rice and Miss Robinson "locked horns" (as Audrey Cole put it) over the three sculptural portraits over the north entrance—the Wesley Family. Miss Robinson planned to have Bishop Coke in place of Susanna Wesley, but Dr. Rice won out. "Everyone including Miss Robinson is glad Susanna is there. By every right she deserves to be. She spent herself preparing her two sons for their mission in life. Second, some woman should be there to represent what women have meant to Methodism. Who is more worthy? Third, the position of woman in modern society demands some recognition. Where could it be shown more appropriately than on a modern Church? Lastly, it is fitting to symbolize the great constructive work that Mrs. Rice has done in the Church," wrote Audrey Cole in "A Twentieth Century Church."

The face of Mrs. Rice's father was used as a model for the "unknown circuit rider," the central figure in the sculptural group over the south entrance. It honors the faithful service of the early circuit riders. The Reverend T.L. Darnell, Mrs. Rice's father, was a circuit rider for most of the fifty-six years of his ministry. The circuit rider is flanked by figures representing Bishop Asbury and Bishop McKendrie, two who were outstanding in Methodist history.

The Kimball organ used in the Fifth and Boston church was

The Fruit of the Spirit is Love...
...eace, Longsuffering, Kindness, Good...
...aithfulness, Meekness, Self-con...

Worship

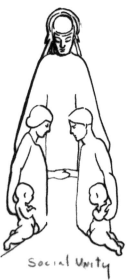

Social Unity

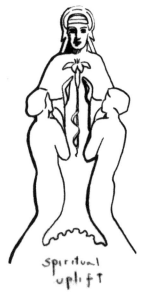

Spiritual Uplift

Indian & Slave Missions

BOSTON AVENUE
UNITED METHODIST
CHURCH

rebuilt, electrified, and moved to the new building to be used in Community Hall where worship services were held from October 1928 to June 1929. Mr. and Mrs. J.R. Cole, Jr., donated a forty-thousand-dollar Kilgen organ for the sanctuary in memory of Mrs. Cole's son Lawrence Bentley, who had sung in the choir for eighteen years.

A Saint Louis firm, Jacoby Art Glass Company, fabricated the stained glass windows that would add so much to the spiritual impact of the church. The stone came from Bedford, Indiana, and the granite from Minnesota.

Correspondence during the two years the building was under construction indicates a great deal of compromise between strong individuals and their ideas, and a considerable amount of supervision and gentle pushing of slow suppliers and craftsmen. One letter from C.C. Cole to Miss Robinson in 1928 said, "We have to stay right in behind Jacoby, even if we have to make half a dozen trips to St. Louis, because these windows, perhaps the most prominent features of the church, just have to be right." At one point, when there was trouble in getting the terra cotta sculptures completed for the south entrance, Miss Robinson went to Chicago, donned overalls, and worked out the details.

There was a price to be paid for all this careful supervision and insistence on highest quality. The cost of the building, originally estimated to be from $500,000 to $750,000, was more than $1,300,000 when completed, including the land and furnishings. Pledges from members were required to make up the difference, but such pledges were not hard to secure in Tulsa in the late 1920s.

The years during which the Thirteenth and Boston church was constructed were boom years. The early optimism of the city fathers and mothers had been more than fulfilled in the first three decades of the twentieth century, with the discovery of oil and the rapid economic development which came with it. In 1928, the city's industrial output totalled $113 million, with $64 million of that in petroleum products, $9 million in derricks, rigs and tanks, and $5 million in oil field supplies. Fortunes were being made every day, it seemed, and some of the most fortunate were happy to contribute to the construction of the new church.

"A story of the Church would be incomplete without the mention of the McFarlin-Chapman-Barnard family who have given generously of their funds to make this building possible," Audrey Cole wrote. "It is beautiful justice that they are giving back to God and to this country a goodly sum of the money with which God thru this country has blessed them. They have been represented on the building committee by Mr. Barnard, a fine character, and by Mrs. Walter who is equally so; the later has rendered invaluable service as chairman of the committee on the interior."

TERRA COTTA

THE THREE SCULPTURES SHOWN ON THE FACING PAGE REPRESENT SPIRITUAL LIFE, RELIGIOUS EDUCATION, AND WORSHIP. BELOW ARE SKETCHES BY ADAH ROBINSON.

THE BUILDING
THE ORIGINAL STRUCTURE

The church building which has attracted worldwide attention for so many years is, indeed, unique. One of the few art deco churches in the nation, it is designed to express the vitality of the Christian faith, and symbolism is used freely. Indeed, the entire structure is symbolic of modern Christian ideas.

Encompassing 150,000 cubic feet, the exterior is of Bedford limestone, steel and terra cotta. The straight, vertical lines of the exterior suggest a church reaching toward God. The tower's four shafts of glass are angled to receive and reflect light. Praying hands found in key places on the exterior of the building are open, symbolic of receiving God's love.

The tower, which Dr. Rice insisted must be a part of the church but must not be a steeple, rises 258 feet. The sanctuary, which so shocked the pastor and the building committee at first, is round and has neither a center aisle nor one main door. The pulpit is central in actuality as well as in spirit. A mosaic was originally planned for the wall behind the pulpit and choir lofts. Because of a lack of funds, it was never executed. In 1961 a mosaic would be designed and installed where the original had been planned.

The Epworth Chapel, which has come to be known as the Rose Chapel, contains some of the most beautiful of the church's many stained glass windows. These unusual rose-tinted windows—Adah Robinson's use of color at its best, according to one source—give the chapel its nickname. The chapel, along with the adjoining parlor, was destined to be used for countless weddings, christenings, and funerals through the years.

Community Hall, on the first floor directly below the main auditorium, was built with a well-equipped stage, and has no fixed seating in order to be flexible for many types of events. The adjoining large kitchen, state of the art at the time in both construction and equipment, was welcomed by Boston Avenue women who had struggled with the tiny and inadequate kitchen in the Fifth and Boston church.

The sanctuary, chapel, and Community Hall all were originally equipped with organs. The sanctuary's forty-eight-rank Kilgen organ

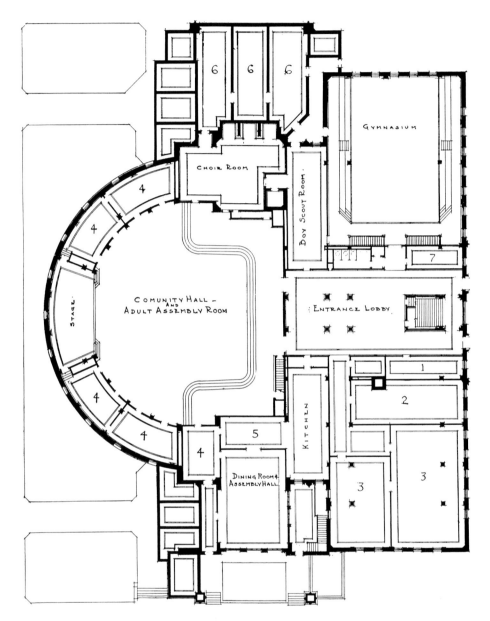

First Floor

1. Nursery	4. Adult Class Rooms
2. Cradle Roll	5. Service Kitchen
3. Beginners	6. Storage Rooms

7. Physical Director
Community Lounge—East Entrance Lobby

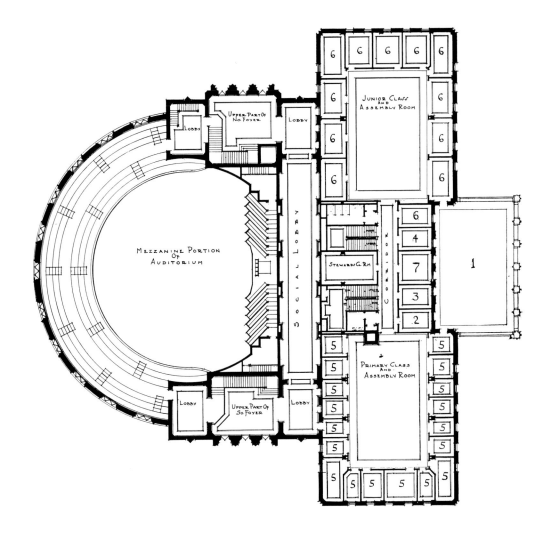

Third Floor

1. ROOF GARDEN
2. KITCHENETTE
3. SECRETARY'S OFFICE

4. COAT ROOM
5. PRIMARY CLASS ROOMS
6. JUNIOR CLASS ROOMS

7. ASSISTANT SUPERINTENDENT'S OFFICE

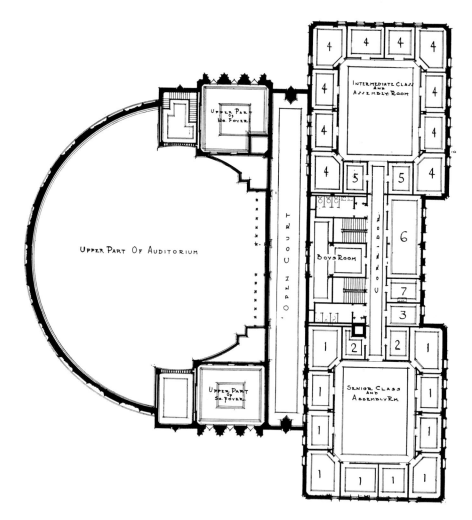

Fourth Floor

1. SENIOR CLASS ROOMS
2. COAT ROOMS
3. KITCHENETTE

4. INTERMEDIATE CLASS ROOMS
5. COAT ROOMS
6. CLUB ROOMS

7. SECRETARY'S OFFICE

**ANGLED ARCHES AND AN
UNUSUAL SOCIAL LOBBY**

THE DISTINCTIVE ANGLED ARCHES
"SUGGEST THE BLESSINGS OF GOD
ON ALL WHO PASS BENEATH." THIS
ARCHED FORM IS USED THROUGHOUT
THE CHURCH FOR DOORS,
WINDOWS, ETCHED GLASS, AND THE
DETAILING OF THE BRASS HARDWARE.
THE SOCIAL LOBBY, BELOW, WAS
CONSIDERED AN UNUSUAL FEATURE
IN A MODERN CHURCH. ITS SOARING
HEIGHT SUGGESTS THE INFINITE
POSSIBILITIES OF HUMAN KINDNESS
AND FELLOWSHIP. LIGHT IS MANIFEST
IN THE OPEN SPACE, THE STAINED
GLASS SKYLIGHTS, AND THE
ATMOSPHERIC COLOR. MOSAICS
WERE ORIGINALLY PLANNED FOR THE
RECESSED PANELS IN THE NORTH AND
SOUTH ENDS OF THE LOBBY.

controlled by a four-manual console was outstanding, and a two-manual Kilgen organ served the chapel. The rebuilt Kimball organ from the old building was used in Community Hall.

The spacious social lobby was an unusual feature for a church of the time, and one for which Dr. Rice fought strenuously. This wide corridor which connects the four-story educational portion of the building to the sanctuary was designed to be a meeting place for the congregation before and after church. Its soaring ceiling inset with glorious stained glass skylights makes it a space of serenity and beauty. Mosaics were originally planned for the walls at each end of the social lobby; because of limited funds, they would not be added until the centennial of the church in 1993.

The original 125 rooms of the church

included offices, classrooms, and assembly rooms. The gymnasium, with separate facilities for boys and girls, was another unusual feature for its time. Many a basketball game was played there before it was renovated to become a choir room and a multi-purpose room in the early 1950s.

The tower, containing eight rooms, each with 20 x 28 feet of usable space, was left unfinished for future expansion. Stairways provided access for cleaning and maintenance.

On the east side of the church building, a porte cochere made Boston Avenue Church one of the first in the nation to accommodate the automobile in its planning. The parking lot, termed "ample" at the time, was another unusual accommodation for automobiles. A roof garden, or terrace, over the porte cochere was used frequently in hot summers before air conditioning.

Adah Robinson called light the primary symbol of the church. More than 11,500 square feet of leaded glass and stained glass windows flood the church with sunlight during the daytime. Downward flowing lines, exemplifying divine light and the

outpouring of God's love, start above the windows and continue from stone into stained glass.

Angled arches over the entrances and throughout the building symbolize the blessing of God upon those who pass beneath. Seven pointed stars used above the entrance and over the windows represent the seven virtues: patience, purity, knowledge, long-suffering, kindness, love, and truth.

Two flowers indigenous to Oklahoma, the tritoma and the coreopsis, are symbols of vital, growing Christianity. The tritoma, or torch lily, grows in shadowed places, a flower of flaming color. Its strong stem signifies the strength of the church and the unusual downward blossoms represent the generosity of the faith. The coreopsis flourishes in the driest, hardest soil, and indicates the hardiness and joy of the Christian faith.

In the booklet "A Twentieth Century Church" the building committee stated that the main auditorium, including the balcony, would accommodate two thousand people and that the capacity of Community Hall was twelve hundred. The capacity of the chapel was estimated to be two hundred fifty. Members of later building committees agree that these figures were a bit generous, and indeed, the original building committee concluded their statement by saying that the church was already expanding and finding the new quarters none too large.

DETAIL OF ADAH ROBINSON'S DRAWING FOR STAINED GLASS WINDOWS
ADAH ROBINSON'S DRAWING WAS SIGNED AND DATED "APRIL 17 '25."

CHAPTER 10

THE CHURCH'S NEW HOME

DR. CLAUDE M. REVES — 1927-1931

Although Dr. Rice's name is engraved on the cornerstone of the "modern cathedral" at Thirteenth and Boston, he was no longer preacher in charge at Boston Avenue Church when construction was completed. The planning of the church had taken its toll on his health, and in 1927 he left Boston Avenue to become editor of the *Oklahoma Methodist Journal.*

The newspaper had been founded in 1921 and edited since by David Holmes Aston. Early in 1927, Aston was married, and then just one month later he suddenly died. Dr. Rice hired his widow Elizabeth Aston for the position of church secretary after her husband's death.

Rice's successor at Boston Avenue was Dr. Claude M. Reves, a graduate of the University of Arkansas and the divinity school at Vanderbilt University, who came to Boston Avenue from Little Rock. He had served as pastor in several Arkansas Methodist churches since entering the ministry in 1908 and had married Ethyl Beloate in 1906. They had one son, Charles Beloate Reves. Dr. Reves had served as a chaplain in the U.S. Army in France from 1917 to 1919.

When he arrived, ground for the new building had been broken, the educational building was well along, and the foundation was staked out for the sanctuary. The old building at Fifth and Boston had been sold to Waite Phillips for $110,000, but he allowed the congregation to continue using it, rent free, for the two years following the sale. He also, unasked, contributed five thousand dollars to the building fund. On that site, Phillips would build the Philcade building, later renamed the Pan American Building. That same year, the Phillips mansion, Philbrook, was completed.

At the final service in the Fifth and Boston church, a special offering was taken for the retired minister's fund, called the superannuate's endowment. The church had finally become aware of the sad financial condition of some of the retired ministers who had given their lives to the church, but had little money accumulated when the time came that they could no longer serve. At that same service, Dr. Reves announced the plans for the move the following Sunday.

Moving day came on October 21, 1928. The entire

congregation marched down Boston Avenue in a procession from Fifth Street to Thirteenth and occupied Community Hall and the educational building, which were sufficiently complete to be used. That date happened to be the birthday of C.C. Cole, chairman of the building committee. Also that day, John Colbert became the first baby baptized in the new building.

Assisting in the move to Thirteenth and Boston were members of the Women's Missionary Society, including the Mms. J.F. and T.E. Smiley, C.J. and J.J. Allen, L. Cooley, Theodore Cox, Frank Martin, Melvin Sutherland, and Bert Hodges, as well as Georgia Fry, Mary Catron, and Mabel Schiek. Mrs. Vivian Kelly volunteered to take charge of the new kitchen, and the society continued making money serving dinners to help pay for the mortgage. After Mrs. Kelly moved away, Mrs. Frank Martin took over and received the title of church hostess and a small salary.

The women's organizations were united and Mary Lou (Mrs. Bert) Hodges, became president of the combined group. After her death, Bert and Bert Junior helped make some things possible for the kitchens that she had wanted, and an engraved plaque was placed on the door in her memory.

The church offices were on the second floor, and for the following eight months, Dr. Reves worked amid dust, pounding of hammers, clutter of floors being laid, and the noise of terrazzo being polished. Bob and Leita Bradshaw would later recall that they had to walk construction planks in November, 1927, to reach the pastor's office to be married. Dr. Reves pushed the financial drive along to help pay for the church.

Mrs. C.C. Cole wrote of Dr. Reves, "No one of the original planners among our members had a more genuine appreciation of the design than he, except such a rare being as Mr. Raymond Courtney who has studied it intensely over a long span of years.

Epworth Chapel, called the Rose Chapel so often that few people know its official name, saw its first wedding on January 10, 1929, when Elizabeth Rice, daughter of Dr. and Mrs. John Rice, became the bride of Robert L. Carruthers. Her father officiated, and the guests sat on folding chairs. Dr. Adah Robinson had stayed up all night the night before the wedding completing a plaster of paris frieze at the top. It was supposed to be replaced by wood later, but was so satisfactory, it was never replaced. Another Elizabeth, daughter of the C.C. Coles, was a flower girl in the wedding.

Miss Robinson later designed the interiors of both the First and Second Christian Science churches in Tulsa. Her background was broad and cultured, including a grandfather who was a stonemason and a sculptor. She also designed a monument to Shakespeare, one of only four in the nation. One of Tulsa's few art deco monuments, it was placed in Woodward Park near Twenty-first and Peoria, and later

moved elsewhere in the park. Miss Robinson later taught at Trinity University in San Antonio, Texas, but returned to Tulsa to retire.

On June 9, 1929, the completed building was occupied and consecrated, and the second Sunday in June has since been considered the building's birthday.

The festivities began with communion at 6:30 on Sunday morning, and would continue for three days. Bishop H.A. Boaz offered the prayer on Sunday morning, and Dr. Louis S. Barton led the responsive reading. Dr. John Rice's sermon was entitled "Ye Are My Witnesses." A special service was held on Sunday afternoon for baptism of infants, reception of new members, and presentation of the American flag. Bishop Boaz gave the sermon on Sunday evening.

The stage in Community Hall was dedicated Monday evening and a two-act comedy presented by the young people. On Tuesday, the building committee and official members held a reception for all who wished to see the building. Festivities concluded Wednesday evening with an organ recital by the nationally known organist from Cleveland, Ohio, Mr. Albert Riemenschneider.

The church was open to the public "for anyone who doesn't

THE ROSE CHAPEL
THE ROOM'S SIMPLICITY OF DESIGN CONVEYS PEACE AND SPIRITUAL REPOSE. THE WINDOWS, RICH IN COLOR AND DELICATE IN DESIGN, JUSTIFY THE NAME OF THE SPECIAL SANCTUARY. THREE CARVED FIGURES ON THE ORGAN SCREEN DENOTED THE CHAPEL'S FUNCTIONS — MEDITATION, CEREMONY, AND WORSHIP. PROCESSIONAL FIGURES ALTERNATING WITH TRITOMA ON THE FRIEZE EXPRESS DEVOTION. CROSSES IN THE STAINED GLASS WINDOWS AND ON THE SOLID GUM WOOD PANELS ARE REMINDERS OF THE CHRISTAN FAITH.

THE SANCTUARY

SYMBOLS ARE USED IN THE STAINED GLASS, ORNAMENTAL PLASTER, OAK WOOD, AND DESIGN OF THE SANCTUARY. FOUR MASSIVE DOORS AND MULTIPLE AISLES SPEAK OF THE ACCESSIBILITY OF GOD. ALL LINES LEAD TO THE PULPIT AND FOCUS ON THE MESSAGE. THE TRITOMA MOTIF IS USED IN BANDS ON THE CHOIR STALL AND PULPIT. TWO CARVED FIGURES BEHIND THE ORGAN CONSOLE REPRESENT WORSHIP AND PRAYER. ON THE MAJESTIC DOME OF THE SANCTUARY CEILING IS A CIRCLE, ANCIENT SYMBOL OF THE INFINITE, WITHOUT BEGINNING AND WITHOUT END. IN THE CENTER OF THE STAINED GLASS IS ANOTHER VARIATION ON THE COREOPSIS FLOWER.

have a place to meet," and would host such diverse events as graduation ceremonies for the Hillcrest Hospital School of Nursing, Hyechka Club recitals, and square dancing.

The Outlook, Boston Avenue's church paper, announced in September of 1929 that "A Twentieth Century Church," a descriptive and illustrated booklet of the new church, had been issued and was available for fifty cents a copy. It contained the story of the building of the church by Audrey Rudd Cole, a statement by the building committee, a message from Dr. John A. Rice, and a description of the building and its symbolism by Miss Adah Robinson.

The Outlook was abandoned the following month, and members began receiving the Boston Avenue Methodist Church edition of the *Tulsa Herald.* The headline on October 18 announced that membership in the church was nearing two thousand.

Members of the congregation who were hard of hearing had a device called an Acousticon available to them, with five receivers in the sanctuary. Scoutmasters Thomas Clement of Troop 20 and Thomas Gannaway of Troop 39 were building up their scout troops, and Sunday morning services were broadcast periodically on KVOO

Radio. Other news of the time included the dedication of Rudd Park at Spavinaw Lake where Betty Cole, the granddaughter of A.J. Rudd, unveiled a tablet commemorating his contributions as water commissioner for the city.

Dolly (Mrs. Russell) Finch remembered that first winter in the nursery, "We had between six and eight infants, and sixty crib babies up to the age of three years. Getting all those little bodies in and out of the old-fashioned snowsuits was quite a job!"

Mrs. Roy Lundy was in Morningside Hospital that winter, recovering from a broken ankle. She was the former Ola Garner from Gravely, Arkansas, and had married Roy Belmont Lundy in 1901. They came to Tulsa in 1910 and were long-time members of the church. He served for many years on the official board, and she was very active in the Women's Society.

Dr. Alfred F. Smith of Nashville, Tennessee, editor of the *Nashville Christian Advocate* and a former pastor of Boston Avenue Church, returned to speak in two services in October. He and Mrs. Smith were the guests of Mr. and Mrs. Lee Clinton.

And so the congregation settled into its stunning new home at Thirteenth and Boston. But the stock market crash in the last days of October, 1929, marked the end of Tulsa's long boom era. The crash and subsequent depression would demolish fortunes in Tulsa, as everywhere across the country, and erase thousands of jobs. For Boston Avenue, it would mean almost losing the beautiful new building. No church exists in a vacuum, and when businesses collapse and jobs disappear, people struggle for simple survival. Church building pledges, which had provided much of the funding for the new building, became impossible for many to fulfill.

In November, 1929, the conference returned Dr. Reves to Boston Avenue for another year. In his Pastor's Message in the *Boston Avenue Church Herald,* he said:

> It is my joy to be your pastor for another year. I cannot tell you how grateful I am for such a privilege as this. I began my year's work with the feeling that no minister is more to be congratulated than I am. I am supremely happy in the blessing that has come to me.
>
> But I am not unmindful of the fact that I have a great task ahead of me. My position as your pastor brings with it heavy responsibilities. I know that I am called not to enjoy an honor but to render the service. And I accept the challenge which comes to me. Already I have purported in my heart to make this year the best in all my ministry.

L.F. Sensabaugh was director of religious education and Dr. P.P. Claxton was Sunday school superintendent as hard financial times set in at Boston Avenue Church. Tom B. Matthews was financial secretary and Mrs. Hugh Robertson was assistant secretary. Salary money went first to cover custodian's salaries, and for other salaries if there was enough money available.

"People don't appreciate how gravely in debt we were . . . we almost lost the church," Mrs. Aston would later report. She and Mrs. Huggins, the church financial secretary, bought their own pencils with their own money. She made an arrangement with an official of the church's bank so that, if there wasn't enough money in the church's account to cover the custodian's salary, she could overdraw for one month. The Missionary Society Christmas Bazaar raised over six hundred dollars, enabling the group to pay one thousand dollars on its building fund pledge.

Tulsa's population in 1930 was 142,000, and the city boasted thirty-seven buildings that stood from ten to twenty stories, and two that were over twenty stories. Looking north on Main Street from Second Street, billiard parlors were numerous. Vaudeville houses, loan companies, rooming houses, talking picture shows, and a barber college lined the street, with the old Brady Hotel looming in the background.

Even as church funds were shrinking, the membership continued to grow. During the four years of Dr. Reves' pastorate six hundred members were added to the church.

CHAPTER 11

DEPRESSION YEARS

DR. CHARLES C. GRIMES - 1931-1934

D r. Charles C. Grimes, the son of a Missouri Methodist minister, became the pastor of Boston Avenue Methodist Episcopal Church South in 1931. He had attended college in Missouri and then at Vanderbilt University, and was married to the former Hannah Troy.

After serving several churches in Missouri, he was presiding elder of the Memphis district and then pastor of the Trinity Methodist Church in Memphis until 1929. He served the Church Street Methodist Episcopal Church South in Knoxville from 1929 until coming to Boston Avenue.

A Knoxville church publication congratulated Tulsa on securing the services of Dr. Grimes, saying, "His character, warmed with human sympathy at the bottom and reaching to heights of lofty austerity at the top, is rare. It is lighted by humor that is natural and unforced. His religion, plainly deeply felt by himself, cannot help but be deeply felt by others. Here is a man with whom to come in contact is to be made spiritually and morally better."

The Church Street Church was a university church and Dr. Grimes was popular with young people on campus. He took a leadership role in completion of a beautiful new church after the previous building burned.

He also was an organizer of great ability, as the Boston Avenue Church members soon would learn. During the depression, social life revolved around the church. There were boys' and girls' basketball teams with games in the much-loved gymnasium on Saturday nights. A Christmas bazaar featured a turkey dinner for fifty cents, plus a fashion show and program. Mr. and Mrs. C.C. Herndon gave the church a radio set that could be moved from room to room because the church had been borrowing one so that the Mothers' Club and other parent groups could hear lectures on the problems of child training.

When diphtheria broke out among the children of the city, church schools suffered a slump in attendance. L.F. Sensabaugh, director of the church school, said, "Strange, is it not, how safe it is to take children to a crowded 'movie,' and how dangerous for them to attend a well-ventilated and sunshine-filled church school room?" But many did come, and Dolly Finch reported that in the nursery room she often had to stand John Colbert, Forrest Darrough, Jr., and a couple of others in the corner when they starting swinging at each other.

However, life had changed dramatically for individuals and for the church. Soup lines were commonplace, and the best jobs for the seven thousand unemployed in Tulsa paid three dollars a day for a three-day work week. When the word spread that timber cutting jobs were available on Bird Creek, 130 men tramped eight miles through snow to seek the jobs.

Of the $1,360,000 that the church had cost, $1,060,000 had been raised and paid. That left $300,000 to be raised, an amount which had seemed to pose no difficulty in the prosperous years of 1927 and 1928 when the debt was incurred. A loan had been arranged and installments set when business conditions seemed to justify the belief that the payments of $43,000 a year were conservative. Now, as the economic depression deepened, it became ever more difficult for the church to make its mortgage payments.

The *Church Herald* headline on April 15, 1931, was "Will Boston Avenue Church be Foreclosed?" The story told of the night and day work of the committee to raise the funds needed, and of those who couldn't afford it but gave anyway—and of those who could afford it that didn't. A junior board of stewards had been organized, and its members were commended for taking an active part in the financial campaign.

As the depression years progressed, it became clear that, despite heroic efforts, the church could not meet the obligation. A special committee was named by the board of stewards to represent the church with the Lincoln National Life Insurance Company, which held the mortgage and was about to foreclose. Hunter L. Johnson, former chairman of the official board and vice president of the finance committee, chaired that committee.

Something had to be done to stop the foreclosure. Johnson and several committee members traveled to Lincoln, Nebraska, to discuss the situation with the insurance company.

Hats in hand, the committee arrived at the offices of the insurance company and began negotiations to work out a refinance of the loan on terms the church could afford. They pled the case for the congregation and offered an alternative to foreclosure. Officials at Lincoln Life were hesitant, but Hunter Johnson clinched the deal with a simple question: "What would you do with a church, anyway?" Apparently the the Lincoln Life officials didn't know, because they agreed to refinance the loan. Church trustees, E.B. McFarlin, C.C. Cole, Judge L.M. Poe, V.P. Rader, Dr. W.M. Wilson and the Lincoln

National Life Insurance Company signed an extension of the loan for a period of ten years from April 1, 1933. At that time the amount refinanced was $321,654.25, which included the unpaid interest.

The first two years, only $9,721.99 was to be paid, and the church would be charged only three percent on the loan for the next two years. (The original loan had been at six percent.) The congregation, now 2,200 members strong, was asked to meet this new obligation. "Of course, members should subscribe in proportion to their ability," their pastor told them, "for always many will unfailingly feel they cannot give anything or they will neglect the matter."

J.R. Simpson, chairman of the finance committee, told the church, "The membership should feel greatly indebted to Mr. Johnson for his leadership." Hunter Johnson's response was, "There is nothing to say about my work." Even later, Johnson had words of gratitude, rather than self-aggrandizement. "When our church shall be accomplishing its destiny in future generations, on tablets to commemorate its growth, personally I think that one tablet should bear this memorial, 'The official building loan of the church was carried by the Lincoln National Life Insurance Company.'"

When the matter was resolved, one relieved member of the congregation said, "We've heard a lot about the depression, but the members of this church aren't depressed now."

Individually, many members were hit hard by the depression. The Cole families were among those who lost much of what they had built over the years. J.R. and C.C. Cole, brothers who had been so instrumental in much of the church's growth, were in the mining business. They had pooled their money and established the Acme Lead and Zinc Mining Company in 1903. Over the years they formed other companies and were involved in real estate and in supporting the growth of the town.

C.C. Cole had become a member of Kiwanis, a trustee of Kendall College, and in 1909, was on the board of the first YMCA. His office was in the Cole Building at Fifth and Boston, and he was on the board of the First National Bank, helped found the Tulsa Chamber of Commerce, and pledged five thousand dollars on the 1928 Stud Horse Note which enabled the Tulsa Municipal Airport to be built.

But the depression brought disaster. The Acme mines were shut, the Coles' property foreclosed, and their servants let go. J.R. was forced to declare bankruptcy and couldn't complete his pledge to the church for which he had worked so hard since 1904. He and his wife moved to New Mexico soon after.

C.C.'s commitment to his church remained as strong as it had been in the heyday of his financial success. Knowing that the church needed the money he had pledged in order to pay its mortgage, he and Mrs. Cole determined to pay both their own pledge and J.R.'s.

AUDREY AND C.C. COLE

Ultimately it came down to a choice between saving their home, Rockmoor, from foreclosure or helping save the church building. They chose to pay the pledges. The family moved into one of their rent houses at Seventeenth and Detroit, and the bank foreclosed on Rockmoor as well as C.C.'s office building downtown.

There is a story, long part of the lore at Boston Avenue Church, which sums up C.C. Cole's attitude toward his losses and the church. As the story goes, the financially struggling Cole was walking along Boston Avenue one day during the depression, discussing his financial difficulties with a friend. Suddenly the friend pointed toward the magnificent building at the end of the avenue and asked him, "Don't you wish now you hadn't given all that money to the church?" Cole looked at his friend in amazement. "Are you kidding?" he said. "That's the best money I ever spent!"

Indeed, the Boston Avenue congregation drew comfort and inspiration from their church during these hard times. The preaching they heard there was as fine as the music and worship setting provided by the beautiful building. A letter received by the C.C. Coles from a church member in Knoxville had indicated this would be so. "Dr. Grimes is the best preacher I have ever heard," the Knoxville member wrote. "His sermons are intellectual, spiritual and very interesting. His philosophy is refreshing, and it gives one something to get hold of."

BABIES MILK FUND FOUNDERS. FROM LEFT TO RIGHT, MRS. H. H. COPPLE, MRS. HUNTER JOHNSON, MRS. EARLE PORTER, MRS. A. W. PIGFORD, AND MISS OLIVE VICKERY. THE PICTURE WAS TAKEN IN 1941, AFTER THE DEATH OF MRS. W. W. MCCLURE, THE SIXTH FOUNDER.

BOSTON AVENUE
UNITED METHODIST
CHURCH

In 1933, the *Tulsa Church Herald* printed a letter from former pastor Percy Knickerbocker, saying "You certainly have a marvelous preacher in Dr. Grimes, one of the very best in the South. I don't know of any I had rather listen to."

Even though times were hard in Tulsa in the early thirties, construction of new buildings didn't stop. Many of these projects, including the Union Depot, the Philcade, expansion of the federal building, and the municipal airport, were funded by the WPA. An art deco style Public Market was constructed at Eleventh and Elgin during that period. Here housewives could make their selections from live chickens on display, then wait while they were killed and cleaned.

Not everyone could afford to buy food, however, and even though they were hard-pressed by the economy, Boston Avenue members didn't blind themselves to the needs of those around them. From early days, the women of Boston Avenue Church had done an outstanding job of determining what needs existed and developing ways to meet those needs. In 1934 the Christian Social Relations Committee of the Women's Society of the church did a study and uncovered the fact that no provisions were made in any existing social agencies for a continued milk supply to babies in need. In January 1935, six members of that committee established the Babies Milk Fund: Mrs. W.W. McClure, Mrs. H.H. Copple, Mrs. Hunter Johnson, Mrs. Earl S. Porter, Mrs. A.W. Pigford, and Miss Olive Vickery. They committed to providing milk every day for a year for babies with no other means of getting it. Departments in the church contributed enough money to start with six babies. This amounted to ten cents a day, or people could commit to thirty-six dollars a year for a baby. Through income from churches, clubs, individuals and by holding one benefit a year, they expanded this effort enormously and continued to help supply milk for Tulsa babies for the next forty-two years.

At the close of Dr. Grimes' four years at Boston Avenue, it was said "We can never outgrow what his ministry has meant to the people of Boston Avenue Methodist Church and the City of Tulsa. He was committed to Christian education. Because of his imprint upon this congregation, it can never turn back to the methods of yesterday and attempt to use outworn and antiquated methods."

The little book, *Boston Avenue Methodist Church, 50 Years,* commented, "Dr. Grimes' strength and power held the church on course during the critical period of the Great Depression."

CHAPTER 12

BROTHER FORNEY

REVEREND FORNEY HUTCHINSON - 1934-1939

The title the Reverend Forney Hutchinson preferred was "Brother Forney." But when the Reverend John Milton Glen Douglas, the minister who baptized him, asked the little boy, "What is your name?" the boy answered, "Forney." Then Douglas asked, "Forney what?" "Forney's all," came the reply. So the youngster was baptized "Forney's All."

He was born in 1875 at Center Point, Arkansas, joined the church at the age of eleven, decided at age fifteen that he would become a minister, and was licensed to preach at the age of twenty. "It was a very definite impulse with me, so definite that I never considered any other life work," he said.

He earned an A.B. degree from Hendrix College in Arkansas and later was a pastor in Little Rock. He went back to school to gain his Bachelor of Divinity degree from Vanderbilt University, which he did in 1905. He then returned to Hunter Memorial Church in Little Rock where he met and, in 1908, married Bertie Anderson. They would have three sons and a daughter: Forney Jr., Kelsey, Paul, and Virginia.

He served churches in Fayetteville, Little Rock, and Texarkana, Arkansas, and then became pastor of Saint Luke's at Oklahoma City in late 1918. Hutchinson had first been assigned to Boston Avenue Church in 1927, but the members of Saint Luke's mounted such a vigorous protest at losing him, he stayed. He remained there until 1932, when he was transferred to the Mount Vernon Place Methodist Church in Washington, D.C.

Information related by Hunter Johnson indicates in what high esteem the Reverend Forney Hutchinson was held. When Johnson was striking his bargain with the insurance company in Nebraska, one of the board members asked him if he knew the Reverend Forney Hutchinson. Johnson replied that the Reverend Hutchinson had been his pastor at St. Luke's Methodist Church in Oklahoma City. The board member advised that if he could persuade the Reverend Hutchinson to come to Boston Avenue as minister, he could help with the monumental fund-raising task.

The Reverend Hutchinson had returned to Arkansas as

presiding elder after leaving Washington, D.C., and it was there that the committee from Boston Avenue Church came to see him. The bishop advised that he would not ask him to accept the pastorate at Boston Avenue because of his health, the fact that he was nearing the end of his illustrious career, and the enormity of the task he would be facing in Tulsa.

But Brother Forney determined that this was a call from God. He would answer the call on one condition. The church—though strapped for funds and deeply in debt—must agree to support a missionary. The committee agreed, and he accepted the pastorate in 1934.

Not long after his arrival in Tulsa, the Reverend Hutchinson made a presentation to the board of stewards, urging that they not delay in making good on the committee's promise to support a missionary. Giving, he explained, was essential to receiving, and providing a witness to the Gospel in the mission field was essential to the vitality of Boston Avenue Church, which had itself begun as a mission forty years before. Hutchinson's specific proposal was that the church provide one thousand dollars a year to support a young missionary to Cuba, Paul Mitchell, an Oklahoman.

A bargain was a bargain, and so the board agreed to support the mission. With this new challenge, the focus of the congregation broadened from simply paying off the building debt to a growing ministry, reaching out to other parts of the world. History has shown the wisdom of Forney Hutchinson's insistence on missions. Economic conditions in Tulsa remained difficult for years, but the church was able to support its missionary and still pay the debt on the the building. Martha Jo Bradley, daughter of Mr. and Mrs. H.H. Copple, would later recall, ". . . Forney Hutchinson was the best person I ever saw. It was due to him that we began sponsoring missionaries to foreign countries. He said 'I know you can't figure out where the money is coming from to sponsor a missionary, but if you do that, it will come.' It did." Since that time, Boston Avenue Church has always had an active foreign mission outreach, and this giving spirit has been a guiding principle for the church.

The Reverend Hutchinson was a minister who liked to see conversions in his church. His congregations were always made up of more converts than the average. He said, "These days, membership comes mostly by letters and taking children into the church. While deeply appreciative of all this, a man grows hungry to see conversion like in other days."

Hutchinson apparently was a man who made an impression on people. Elizabeth Smith, daughter of Dr. W.M. Wilson, remembers him coming down into the congregation during church services and singing a hearty version of "That Old Time Religion." (Rumor said he did that when he felt the congregation wasn't paying close enough attention to the sermon.) The Reverend Hutchinson said he sometimes was tempted to be critical when people were not measuring up to his standards. "I find it hard to adjust myself to new conditions. Especially am I tempted to be critical of some of our young people. I can't reconcile my ideals for women and girls with cigarette smoking and cocktail parties," he said. He felt the church of that day had too much head and not enough heart.

"I was very unsophisticated about the ministry when I came into it," he recalled. "I thought of ministers as being men apart, rather like angels. I was distinctly honored and flattered that the Lord and the church could use me, and I still am, though I have come to know by now that ministers are as other human beings. I have never lost the impression that I am in the work the Creator intended me to do, though conscious that I never have done it as well as I should."

Tulsa was still in the grip of the depression in 1934, and business owners and bookkeepers, store clerks and delivery men worked side by side with pick and shovel on WPA projects throughout the city. They transformed the wild gulch on South Peoria between the George Snedden Mansion (later the Tulsa Garden Center) and Woodward Park into the Tulsa Rose Garden. The Tracy Park tennis courts at Eleventh and Peoria were a WPA project, as was Mohawk Park. Many men reported to work at Newblock Park and were taken to their WPA jobs by truck.

Norma Smallwood and Tulsa oilman Thomas Gilcrease, who had married in 1928, were divorced that year. Norma's lawyer was

THE BOSTON AVENUE GIRLS' BASKETBALL TEAM, 1934 FRONT ROW, LEFT TO RIGHT: BERNICE RUTH HARE, LEONA GRIGGS, DONNA YEAGER, OLEITA BANKS, AND LOYAL IVERSON. BACK ROW, LEFT TO RIGHT: SARA DONALSON, LOUISE WATSON, RUTH WHITESIDE, E. A. LANDFAIR, LAVONA PARHAM, AND EVELYN WALKER.

Ned Poe, son of Judge L.M. Poe. Ned had joined his father's firm, Poe, Lundy and Morgan, and later would have his own firm, Poe, Murdoch and Langford. Bob Wills and his Texas Playboys were becoming famous across the country for their western swing music, broadcasting live from Cain's Academy of Dancing.

The Coney Island Sandwich Shop next door to the ten story *Tulsa World* building on Boulder offered coneys for a nickel, and the Society for the Preservation of Barbershop Quartet Singing in America was founded in 1935 at the Alvin Hotel.

In 1935 Dr. W.M. Wilson was honored by the congregation for his thirty-six years of service as a trustee of the church. He had been a leading layman for all but the first six years of this congregation's existence.

By this time, the church counted among its members younger men and women who would follow Dr. Wilson's example in giving many years of faithful service to the church. Two such members were the L.C. Clarks. Mr. Clark had come to Tulsa with his family at the age of six and had worked hard to establish himself in Tulsa. First working for twenty dollars a month on the Bynum farm at what would one day be Seventy-first and Memorial, he later found a job in a downtown hardware store. That experience had led him into partnership in the Clark-Darland Hardware Store.

In 1937, L.C. Clark and his wife Sybil helped found the Young Couples Sunday school class. They invited several young married couples to their house for dinner to discuss the possibility of forming

THE BOSTON AVENUE BOYS' BASKETBALL TEAM, 1934. THIS PHOTOGRAPH CAPTURES THE SPIRIT OF THE CHAMPIONSHIP BOY'S BASKETBALL TEAM WITH TROPHIES. IDENTIFICATION ON THE BACK OF THE PHOTO LISTS GENE W. HARE, A NAME THAT CAN'T BE READ, B. BEELER, WALTER DOERING, MELVIN "HATTIE" HATFIELD, RAY HILBURN, G. E. ENGLE, SR., WAYMAN E. HUMPHREY, BILL BILVRO, AND R. C. LANDFAIR.

FELLOWSHIP AND LEARNING
ONE OF MANY INNOVATIVE SUNDAY
SCHOOL CLASSES, THE OXFORD
STUDY CLASS (ABOVE) WAS
ORGANIZED IN THE 1930S. BELOW,
CHURCH MEMBERS WERE
PHOTOGRAPHED AT A 1940S
BANQUET IN COMMUNITY HALL. DR.
H. BASCOM WATTS STANDS AT THE
HEAD TABLE IN THE BACK.

a new class. The next Sunday, forty-five couples showed up in the new class. The first teacher was the Reverend Bentley Sloan, who was the director of Christian education for the church. As they grew older the, the class changed from the "Young Couples" to the Friendly Couples class, and many years later, they became simply the Friendly class.

Devoted church people like the Clarks, who served as sponsors for new young couples Sunday school classes as they were formed, played a key role in the classes' success. "The sponsors' pastoral-type care held the classes together through the formative years," Elizabeth Galloway would later recall. "They did everything they could to help the young couples through the hard times when they were just getting their feet on the ground. Boston Avenue was a big church, but the sponsors provided small church warmth and caring."

Bronze busts of Dr. John Rice, Adah Robinson, and C.C. Cole, the three that were so instrumental in the building of the Thirteenth and Boston church, were unveiled in Community Hall following Sunday morning worship service on June 13, 1937. The inscription on Miss Robinson's read, "Adah M. Robinson, whose creative mind conceived this church, the design, the significance, color symbols; whose courage and patience carried them to completion." Also on display in the library was the mold of the praying hands which adorn the building. The only other mold is in the Museum of Modern Art in New York City.

The day following the dedication of the busts, Dr. Will C. House of Pampa, Texas, pastor of Boston Avenue during Dr. Barton's absence in WWI, was the principal speaker at the All Church Men's Banquet.

A different type of statue met a different end when an attempt to place it in the little triangle just north of the church was squelched by church members in 1937. It was to be a twenty-foot statue of Mae Lilly, the wife of Pawnee Bill, seated on a rearing horse. It is said that L.C. Clark led the battle to keep the statue from being erected.

Tulsa was rocked by a strike at the Mid-Continent Petroleum refinery in 1938. It became so violent the National Guard was called in and stood guard over the refinery with guns, bayonets, and barbed wire. It would not be settled until 1940. Will Rogers High School opened in Tulsa in 1939, sitting in the middle of a field. Students, who had to walk a cow path from Eleventh Street, were warned to look out for the cattle.

L.C. AND SYBIL CLARK IN 1944

"Brother Forney" always said he was just a country preacher at heart. In 1930, when the General Conference in Dallas sought to elect him bishop, he pleaded to remain a pastor, saying "I prefer to live close to my people where I can help them with their problems and encourage them to live as Christians." He said he was not cut out for executive work and had no interest in it.

At Boston Avenue, his sermons became famous. One, preached in 1939 after the congregation had been in the Thirteenth and Boston church for ten years, was entitled "The Gospel According to Boston Avenue." He noted that the church preaches through its tower, in location, majesty, beauty, constancy. "It speaks of God and home and holiness and heaven. It denounces sin with all of its impurity and calls to repentance. Its praying hands are always open toward heaven, and ever there is going forth a call for the weary and the heavy laden to come and find rest." He also said the church preaches through her pews, her pulpit, and her debt, which he called a challenge.

Brother Forney liked to visit in people's homes, but he also visited up and down the street in businesses until health and his eyesight failed. He grieved when he could no longer recognize people on the street. He was much loved by his congregation, and urged not to leave.

Eventually, he decided he must retire, but the Hutchinsons loved Tulsa, and chose to retire here. He was recognized by the congregation at a special Hutchinson Recognition Day during Dr. Galloway's pastorate, and he was presented with a handsome cane.

The Reverend Hutchinson died in 1957 at the age of 81. A memorial written at that time by Mrs. Redmond S. Cole noted that the young and the old, the rich and the poor had been strengthened by his prayers.

Church School, Music, and a Debt Paid

Dr. H. Bascom Watts - 1939-1950

D r. H. Bascom Watts followed the Reverend Hutchinson to the Boston Avenue pulpit in 1939. Like Dr. Barton, he wore a formal morning coat in the pulpit and usually had a rosebud in his lapel. Another native of Arkansas, he was born in Yellville, the son of a Methodist minister, and held his first pastorate at the age of fourteen in Amarillo, Texas. A graduate of Southwestern University at Georgetown, Texas, he earned a Bachelor of Divinity degree from Southern Methodist University in 1918 and was granted an honorary Doctorate of Divinity from Southwestern in 1932.

After serving as pastor of Methodist churches in Waco, Austin, and San Antonio, Texas, and at First Methodist Church in Little Rock Arkansas, he came to Boston Avenue at the age of forty-nine with his wife, Minnie. They had two children, Ewart, who became a minister, and a daughter who was later Mrs. Sterling Wheeler. Called a "brilliant preacher," he memorized all of his sermons, and could repeat them exactly if asked.

In his first report as pastor of this church he wrote, "I very much wish our tower could be lighted every night. The cost seems at present prohibitive, but this beacon of the Christian church along with the rest of Tulsa's impressive skyline is something to be earnestly desired."

Ardently opposed to the repeal of prohibition, he said, "I shall not by my vote become a party to putting a bottle to the lips of the youth of this state."

In 1937, Dr. Watts asked Mr. and Mrs. H.H. Copple to sponsor the Epworth League. Horace Howard Copple was the manager of a shoe department where Miss Johnnye Powell had come to work when she moved to Tulsa. They were married in 1916, and he switched from the Presbyterian Church to the Methodist.

When they began working with college-age young adults in the Epworth League (which later became the Young Adult Sunday school

MR. AND MRS. H.H. COPPLE.
THE COPPLES WERE PHOTOGRAPHED
AT A 1941 CHRUCH RETREAT.

THE EPWORTH LEAGUE

This photo was made at the group's 1936 reunion. Dr. and Mrs. Barton are on the second row at the far right.

class) it had only eight or ten members. They built it up steadily to more than one hundred members. One of the favorite teachers in the class was Mickey Poe, one of the five sons of Judge and Mrs. L.M. Poe.

Mrs. E.E. Clulow, the church organist, died and Mrs. J.H. Englebrecht substituted through 1939 and 1940. Handel's Messiah was first performed in 1939, and would become an Advent season tradition through the years.

The year 1939 brought tremendous changes within the Methodist church. In Kansas City on May 10, the three branches of Methodism adopted a Declaration of Union that healed the divisions which had occurred so many years before. The Methodist Episcopal Church South, the Methodist Protestant Church, and the Methodist Episcopal Church united to become simply the Methodist Church. Nine hundred delegates and fifty bishops were present at the conference at which this momentous step was taken, and the ceremony was concluded with the singing of the "Hallelujah Chorus."

One of the results of the union of the churches was that there was to be only one women's organization, and the Woman's Society of Christian Service was established at Boston Avenue in 1940. Dr. Watts appointed a committee chaired by Mrs. Redmond Cole to study the need and help organize the group. Committee members included Mrs. Hunter L. Johnson, Mrs. W.M. Trotter, Mrs. L.C. Clark, and Mrs. Bert C. Hodges. Mrs. Hodges was the first president, and the other officers elected included Mrs. M.H. Watts, Mrs. Forney Hutchinson, Jr., Mrs. Ernest Rector, Mrs. Hunter L. Johnson, Mrs. Redmond S. Cole, Mrs. S.S. Lawrence, Mrs. Bruce Norman, Mrs. L.C. Clark, Mrs. Harley Lundy, Mrs. Ben Davis, and Mrs. T.E. Smiley. Mr. Roy A. Koons also was a charter member. The Wesleyan Service Guild was allowed to continue, but as an associate of the WSCS.

Mrs. Cole would be a vital part of the WSCS through the years, serving as president of Eastern Oklahoma Conference in 1940. The wife of attorney Redmond S. Cole, she was also a vital part of the Boston Avenue congregation for many years.

A young man joined the church in 1940 who would leave his imprint forever on Boston Avenue's music program. Over the next thirty-two years Marvin Reecher would build one of the largest church music programs in the nation. A native of Hagerstown, Maryland, Reecher had graduated from Westminster Choir College in Princeton, New Jersey. By the time he had been at Boston Avenue nine years, there were eight choirs and the Chancel Choir had gained national recognition, singing several times on the Columbia Church of the Air. By 1963, there were eleven choirs with 555 voices, and they were in demand for concerts throughout Oklahoma.

Camps, banquets, summertime trips to Westminster for choir members, bell choirs, and other programs kept church members old and young involved in bringing God's music into the church. Mrs. Marvin Reecher, the former Helen Bement, was one of the accompanists through the years. Reecher was honored in 1964 at a silver anniversary dinner. He left Boston Avenue in 1972.

The fame of the beautiful church building in Tulsa continued to spread. In 1941 it was featured in *National Geographic Magazine,* and was included in the *Encyclopedia Britannica.* Mrs. John Kolstad, who had served churches in New York City, Chicago, and St. Louis, became the church organist that year.

The United States entered World War II in 1941, and again Tulsans pitched in to do their part. By the time of the church's golden anniversary celebration in late 1943, more than three hundred men and women from the church were serving in the Armed Forces and a U.S.O. unit was based at the church. Patriotic rallies and drives to sell war stamps and war bonds were common in the city.

At the beginning of the war, W.G. Skelly travelled to Washington, D.C., and convinced the War Department that Tulsa was the place to build a massive new bomber assembly plant that was being planned. In 1942, the $45 million Air Force Plant Number 3 became a huge landmark in northeast Tulsa. During the war, Tulsa's Spartan School of Aeronautics trained twenty thousand pilots and five

MRS. REDMOND COLE

thousand mechanics for the air war being fought so bitterly.

H.H. Copple proposed to the board of Christian Education to keep the church open every night with a reading room, games, the gymnasium, etc., to provide wholesome recreational and social activities for the large numbers of young people in town. The board approved and appointed Mr. Copple head of a committee, along with Mrs. Landfair and Judge L.M. Poe, to develop and present a plan.

Forrest M. Darrough was elected chairman of the board of stewards in 1943. By now, membership in the church exceeded 3,700. Eunice Mauzy became the first person in the state to hold the position of director of children's activities for a church. It was a post she would fill for nineteen years. Later Mrs. Mauzy would serve for another nineteen years leading guided tours through the church building following Sunday morning services. Her husband, Judge Whit Mauzy, worked with the Boy Scouts and served on numerous church committees.

The Wesley Fellowship class was formed in 1943, with Harold L. Nichols as the first teacher. A class for young couples, many of whom were returning service men and their wives, it would become a strong supporter of mission projects through the years.

In 1943, Dr. Watts wrote to Mrs. C.C. Cole, following the publication of her book about the history of the first fifty years of the church, congratulating her on the "wonderful service you rendered in writing our history. In my opinion it was both exceptionally well written and an authentically told story. I predict that when the history is written by someone else at the one hundredth anniversary, it will do full justice to the great service to Boston Avenue Methodist Church rendered by both yourself and your esteemed husband."

The South Central Jurisdictional Conference met at Boston Avenue Church in 1944, and W. Angie Smith was elected bishop. When Jane Heard Clinton died that year at the age of seventy, the city lost one of its driving forces in the development of the arts. Dr. Fred S. Clinton would later marry again, and his second wife, Beulah Jane Clinton would give the church a living memorial in his name in 1988. He died in 1955.

THE BOSTON AVENUE CHURCH
SOFTBALL TEAM, 1941

TEAM MEMBERS WERE IDENTIFIED ONLY BY LAST NAME AND THE POSITION THEY PLAYED. FRONT ROW: MOTT, PITCHER; ZEA, CATCHER. SECOND ROW: GOW, SHORTSTOP; McCOLLUM, RIGHT FIELD. THIRD ROW: SMITH, COACH; PRUITT, LEFT FIELD; WELCH, RIGHT FIELD; LUNDY, CATCHER.

The Copples retired as sponsors of the Epworth League at the end of the war. Mr. Copple said it was just too hard to be in the group when so many of the church's fine young men hadn't returned.

Tot (Mary Caroline) Cole, a member of the American Institute of Architects, returned to Tulsa in 1945 to work for Joseph R. Koberling's architectural firm, after leaving a Kansas City firm. She became the first woman architect in the state. Tot had been a teenager during the exciting years of planning and construction on the church building at Thirteenth and Boston, when her parents had worked so closely with Adah Robinson, and this experience had influenced her to become an architect herself. Now, she wanted to work in residential architecture, and Koberling wrote her about a subdivision he and some others had underway near Thirty-first and Harvard. Called the Utopian Subdivision, each lot would face a perimeter road and back up to a lake. She moved into her parents' garage apartment at 1107 Sunset Drive.

No milestone in the church's history was ever celebrated with more joy and gratitude than the one reached in 1946 when the debt on the church building was finally paid off. A gala round of events was held, with a banquet, a city-wide reception, and two services on Sunday highlighting the festivities. Several former pastors returned to celebrate with the congregation, and dozens of church members were pressed into service for the city-wide reception. Mrs. B.A. Mulder, Mrs. John S. Kolstad, E.O. Bennett, Mrs. Hugh Perry, Mrs. B.A. Davis, J.W. Lipscomb, Le Ross Parke, and V. P. Rader were among them.

The Columbia Church of the Air broadcast Bishop Paul E. Martin's early Sunday morning service over more than two hundred

THE CHURCH SERVICE FLAG, WORLD WAR II

SERVICE TO CHURCH AND COMMUNITY
EUNICE MAUZY, LEFT, DIRECTED CHILDREN'S ACTIVITIES AND JANE HEARD CLINTON, RIGHT, WAS A POWERFUL PROPONENT FOR THE ARTS.

radio stations. Then, at the second service, Trustees J.R. Simpson, Chairman C.C. Cole, James H. Gardner, Dr. W.M. Wilson, Theodore Cox, V.P. Rader, E.B. Howard, Summers Hardy, and Bishop W. Angie Smith conducted a ritual of dedication. The mortgage which had once seemed a formidable threat to the church's financial survival was burned at that ceremony. "Burning the mortgage really impressed me," recalled Elizabeth Wilson Smith.

Membership of the church at that time was 4,400. Dr. Bascom Watts reminded the members that it was not "Journey's End," but rather "Pilgrim's Progress." They adopted the slogan, "Freed from debt, not to take it easy; Freed for service, to take it earnestly."

Dr. Watts himself had made no small contribution to the church's freedom for service. Church member and historian Mary Metzel would later recall that "Dr. Watts did a monumental job over a tough time. The church had begun with a building debt of $179,000 and ended debt free during Dr. Watts' pastorate."

Dr. Watts apparently loved pastoring this congregation and was not anxious to leave it, even to take a more prestigous position. According to Mary Metzel, "At the annual conference in 1948, he and Dr. Frank were tied after several rounds of balloting for bishop. Dr. Watts then got up and said that he would like to withdraw his name. He said that Dr. Frank was younger and would have longer to serve the church," she related. Dr. Frank was then elected.

Young families were flocking into the church during these postwar years, and Dr. Watts' leadership was, no doubt, one of the reasons many chose to join Boston Avenue. The Mr. and Mrs. Sunday school class, which would later become the New Covenant class, was formed in October of 1949. Ed and Mildred Day, Ray and Jean Masters, and Bob and Myra Critz were key members at its beginning.

In 1950, Dr. Watts' eleven-year tenure at Boston Avenue Church came to an end. In his farewell message at the fourth quarterly conference that year, Dr. Watts noted that the church had gone from one inferior parsonage to one highly valuable parsonage and one that is fairly satisfactory. The church kitchen was now one of the best equipped available. The job of air conditioning the now-famous twenty-two-year-old building had just been completed. A total of $340,225 had been spent on church property during his time here.

During Dr. Watts' final year at Boston Avenue $36,350 went to such causes as regular World Service apportionments, the missionary special, the Women's Society of Christian Service, the Babies Milk Fund, the Retired Minister's Fund, the district board of mission and church extension, to aiding needy small churches, and to other missions too numerous to list. He said that during the past eleven years $203,923 had been given to missionary and benevolent causes.

"Much of the growth of our church is due to our remarkable

church school. The average attendance during the past year has been 1,300, and enrollment has grown from 2,335 to 3,811. Under the leadership of a fine minister of youth [the Reverend Norton E. Wey], our young people's program has become one of the best in this section. Further, we have developed here one of the great church music organizations of the entire nation.

"While I am reporting on organizations, it is fitting to mention

THE THIRTEENTH AND BOSTON BUILDING

FROM THE FIRST, THE DRAMATIC CHURCH BUILDING HAS BEEN AN IMPORTANT FEATURE OF THE CITY.

The Crusaders," he said. "I am partial to them because I organized them. They represent the strong, gifted manhood of our church, working in the Christ-called mission of visitation evangelism. They make the difference between a church with a mediocre record of recruitment and one that stands at or near the top. In the five years of their existence, they have made 5,500 calls and have brought 1,345 into church membership.

"You have a highly satisfactory two-fold missionary enterprise. Your home missionary project is to contribute largely toward the establishment of new Methodist churches in Tulsa and the vicinity.

"As your special foreign missionary enterprise, you have the support of the Reverend and Mrs. Murray Dickson at Cochabamba, Bolivia. Through the gift of Mr. Howard Allen and our own additional contributions, we have built and furnished a lovely home for them. The investment amounts to about ten thousand dollars. Under Mr. Dickson's leadership, young natives are being trained for Christian service and offer endless opportunity for your investment in scholarship for needy boys and girls and other help."

One of the people instrumental in helping Dr. Watts accomplish all that he did during his last four years at Boston Avenue was Mrs. Mildred Bolds. She "sort of happened into" working at the church when her sister, who was secretary to the Oklahoma Conference secretary, became ill just as the conference was about to meet at Boston Avenue in 1946. Mrs. Bolds filled in and then worked part time at the church when she was needed. In 1948, she began working full time as secretary to Dr. Watts. When he left to become Tulsa district superintendent, she went with him. She returned to Boston Avenue in 1952 when he became a bishop.

Membership in the church almost doubled, going from 2,750 to 5,215 during the eleven years of Dr. Watts' pastorate, and Boston Avenue Church became the seventh largest congregaton in Methodism. His final sermon was attended by two thousand people

THE REVS. WATTS, BALL, AND BARTON
REVS. H. BASCOM WATTS, J. H. BALL, AND L. S. BARTON POSE IN FRONT OF THE CHURCH THEY SERVED AND LOVED SO WELL.

in 1950. He concluded that sermon with these words, "I have loved my work. I have loved my people with an almost worshipful love. You have been all things to me. The very thought of leaving you breaks me all up. To have had the honor and privilege of serving you has been a distinct blessing from heaven."

About the church's growth, Dr. Watts told his beloved congregation, "Sometimes I hear it said, 'Boston Avenue is getting too big.' But, for better or for worse, you must accept the responsibility of bigness. You can't turn the pages back and become a little church. The location, the beauty, the fame, the permanency of this structure call for largeness. The metropolitan character of a great and growing city, with this church as its center, demands it. The reach of your shadow across the city and the nation grows with the years. You can't push back, you must thrust onward. While you must recognize your obligation to help and foster the planting and development of neighborhood Methodist churches throughout the city, you must be aware of your distinct mission as a great and growing church. Littleness has no place in the future of the church. It can only fulfill its calling in an expanding horizon of usefulness."

Bascom Watts was appointed district superintendent over the Tulsa district by Bishop W. Angie Smith when he left Boston Avenue. It came as a complete surprise to him when he was elected bishop on the first ballot in 1952.

Minister and Bishop

Dr. Paul V. Galloway - 1950-1960

D r. Paul V. Galloway, who became pastor of Boston Avenue Church in 1950 at the age of 46, called the people of this church "among the best in the world." Born in 1904 in Mountain Home, Arkansas, he attended Hendrix College in Arkansas and Henderson-Brown College at Arkadelphia. He graduated from Yale Divinity School in 1928.

In 1924, he was licensed to preach while still in college, and became a circuit rider, serving seven little churches in Arkansas. He served as assistant pastor in the First Methodist Church in Fort Smith before entering theology school at SMU. By 1931 he was an elder in the North Arkansas Conference.

After a year in Mexico as a teacher and baseball coach at a mission school, he returned to Arkansas to preach. But after that year, he never lost his zeal for and love of mission work.

In 1932 he was married to Elizabeth Boney and brought his bride to Joyner, Arkansas, to one of his small churches. He said, "She was from a well-to-do family with a home with two or three bathrooms . . . and we had a path out back from our first 'parsonage.' We didn't have running water in the house until we were assigned at Clarendon, Arkansas, and I had my fifth church before we had a house with weights to hold the windows open."

But each assignment was larger than the next. The couple had a son, Paul Jr., and a daughter, Elizabeth Ann, who lived only to the age of seven. Through the years he served as pastor at eight Arkansas churches including Fayetteville for five years and Winfield Methodist in Little Rock, where he was "scouted" by a group from Tulsa.

During the years Dr. Galloway was the pastor at Boston Avenue, the Sunday school attendance was the largest ever—before or since. He thoroughly enjoyed preaching, hospital visiting, and meeting regularly with all age groups within the church for "question and answer" sessions. He was active in the United Fund and the Chamber of Commerce in Tulsa, but spent the majority of his time and effort working with his congregation and in conference work.

The pastors at Boston Avenue Church have always been

supported by a congregation whose members were willing to assume responsibility and work hard for the church. For the positions of responsibility, such as the board of trustees, or the dozens of unsung areas where volunteers are needed within the church, there has always been someone willing to step forward and shoulder the burden. On the board of stewards, George R. Cathey succeeded Forrest Darrough as chairman in 1951, a post he held until 1953. Bob Bradshaw was elected next, and served for three years. Leon and Sue Meigs served as the first presidents of the Homebuilders Sunday school class when it was formed in September of 1954.

L.C. Clark, who was a former chairman of the Boston Avenue board of stewards and chairman of the executive committee, was so active in church work he was thought of in the community as "Mr. Methodist," Elizabeth Galloway would later recall. The minister of another large downtown Tulsa church once told Dr. Galloway, "I'd swap five of my lay leaders for one L.C. Clark."

Clark was the mayor of Tulsa from 1954 to 1956. As mayor, he obtained the right of way from the Katy Railroad for the Broken Arrow Expressway without cost to the city, meeting with railroad officials in their private railroad car parked at the Union Depot to make the arrangements. He also purchased the land for Riverside Airport and acquired the Tulsa Garden Center for the city. He recalled sitting in oilman Bill Skelly's office to negotiate the purchase of the Garden Center for $85,000. Thomas Gilcrease went to Clark with his concerns about what to do to save his art and document collection. Clark promised to do what he could as mayor, and pushed for a $2.25 million city bond issue to buy the collection. The result, of course, is the now world-famous Gilcrease Museum.

Some of Mayor Clark's recommendations and decisions were controversial. He was far ahead of his time in saying that the voters should be able to decide whether they wanted another form of city

CHURCH SCHOOL ATTENDANCE REACHES RECORD HEIGHTS
THE SENIOR HIGHS, TOP, OVERFLOWED THEIR ROOM IN 1957. IN THE CENTER IS A TYPICAL SUNDAY SCHOOL CLASS FROM THE 1950S. AT BOTTOM, YOUNG PEOPLE SING ALONG WITH GAYLE CHRISTENSEN AT THE PIANO.

government, and was harshly criticized for that recommendation.

Another Boston Avenue member succeeded him as mayor in 1956. George Norvell, the twenty-eighth mayor of the city, was the first to hold that office who had been born in Tulsa. Norvell also was the first juvenile judge in Tulsa County and was instrumental in beginning construction of the Skelly Bypass.

Barbara Benefiel, a young woman from Coffeyville, Kansas, became the church organist in 1956, as well as secretary of the music department. She had received a BA in music from Hastings College in Nebraska, studied organ extensively, and earned a master's degree in music composition. In 1956, the church purchased forty-nine new English handbells to begin a bell choir for the junior high school boys whose voices had begun to change. The four-octave set was purchased with donations from individual church members. Five octave sets would be added in 1959 and 1970.

When C.C. Cole died in 1956, former pastor Dr. Reves wrote to Audrey, "His life was gentle, and the elements so mixed in him that Nature might stand up and say to all the world, This was a Man."

In 1957, Dan P. Holmes became

THE 25TH BIRTHDAY OF THE THIRTEENTH AND BOSTON BUILDING
HELPING TO CELEBRATE THE QUARTER-CENTURY MARK IN 1954 WERE, LEFT TO RIGHT, DELPHINE (MRS. J. H.) BALL, MARGUERITE (MRS. JOHN W.) WEBB, BERTIE (MRS. FORNEY) HUTCHINSON, HELEN (MRS. RICHARD) WHITWAM, ELIZABETH (MRS. PAUL V.) GALLOWAY, JANE (MRS. LOUIS) BARTON, AND MINNIE (MRS. H. BASCOM) WATTS.

president of the board of stewards. He had come to Tulsa in 1913 at the age of ten and had sold newspapers to help the family income. When he graduated from Central High School in 1922, his father asked him if he wanted a Model T or money to attend college. He chose the car. "It was a decision I've always regretted," he would say later. He had gone into the insurance business in 1929, and was a

THE BOSTON AVENUE CHOIR

THIS 1950s PHOTOGRAPH WAS TAKEN BEFORE THE REMODELING WHICH INCLUDED THE MOSAIC AND THE CROSS.

DAN. P. HOLMES

long-time trustee of the University of Tulsa. He served on numerous civic boards and supported the community in any way he could.

In his double breasted suit, Holmes became a familiar sight to television audiences, appealing to their sense of civic pride to support one of the many projects that he felt would improve the community. The unusual thing about his sponsorship of television programs and his commercials was that his commercial time was totally given to civic projects. The name of the insurance agency appeared on the screen only at the end of the commercial.

His favorite project, as anyone knows who watched Tulsa television during the fifties, sixties and seventies, was Highway 33, the two-lane blacktop road which connected Tulsa with Fayetteville, Arkansas. His wife's mother had moved to Decatur, Arkansas, and they made the trip many times over a road long in need of improvement. A stretch of that highway, now numbered 412, is named the Dan P. Holmes Expressway in honor of the man who reminded everyone, "Don't forget Highway 33!" week after week in his television advertising. Holmes was also honored at groundbreaking ceremonies for the Cherokee Expressway, a part of the same road. His dream, a good road from Tulsa to Arkansas, was completed after his death in 1983.

When Boston Avenue was made a one-way street going north in 1957, the city was robbed of one of its most beautiful vistas, that of Boston Avenue Church as it was approached from the north. Dr. Galloway was contacted the following year by a book publishing firm in New York preparing to publish a book called Historic Churches of the United States and wanted to include Boston Avenue.

By 1958 Boston Avenue Church services were being televised over Channel 6. The Reverend Duane Murphy, who had worked with the youth program, left that year and the Reverend William D. Bowles replaced him. Race Relations Sunday was held in February 1960 during Interracial and Brotherhood Month, and in March the

THE PORTE COCHERE
THE PORTE COCHERE WAS FILLED WITH HURRYING CHURCH MEMBERS ON SUNDAY MORNING.

church set a goal of two thousand people in attendance for Sunday morning services. The Oklahoma annual conference met at Boston Avenue in May of that year.

The Reverend Murray Dickson, the church's missionary to Bolivia, spoke to the Senior High Department in March of 1960. The work of the Reverend Dickson and his wife Nova was supported in the church by Easter offerings and special fund raising projects by Sunday school classes and other groups. The church provided the Dicksons, who had three children, with a salary of approximately $2,400 a year. He was much loved, and in addition to his official reports to the church, corresponded personally with many members besides. Tragically, Murray Dickson was killed in a car wreck in the 1960s. He was sadly mourned in "his Tulsa church."

BISHOP AND MRS. PAUL GALLOWAY

Dr. Paul Galloway and longtime church member Walton Clinton were "doubles," looking so much alike that people often got them confused, although Clinton was, as he said "a little older and a little taller." The confusion afforded them some wonderful stories, especially since the Channel 6 telecast of Boston Avenue's Sunday service had made Dr. Galloway something of a Tulsa celebrity. One Sunday morning, Clinton had to make a real estate transaction, but first stopped for gasoline at a service station at Eighteenth and Boston. The attendant was obviously perturbed. "Why aren't you in church at Boston Avenue?" he asked. "I had to work," Clinton replied. "Had to work? But you are their preacher and that's where you are supposed to be working," the station attendant insisted.

"Paul was the most popular minister in town," Clinton says of Dr. Galloway (who does have a twin sister). "He was always a good sport when some confused person would slap him on the back and ask about some real estate transaction."

The congregation demonstrated its affection for the Galloways when they presented them with a new Chrysler automobile in 1953.

When he was elected bishop in 1960, he said,"I was amazed. I didn't know that so many of my fellow ministers even knew my name. But I was torn. All I had ever wanted to be was a good minister to my people." But his doubts vanished when he felt a new freshness of call after the beautiful consecration ceremony. "I was available to God to do with as he willed."

His reaction was a typically humble one when he was assigned to the San Antonio-Northwest Texas Area. "When I think of all that territory . . . 226,000 square miles . . . all those people, all those churches . . . and all they have is me! God must help me."

Upon leaving Boston Avenue he said, "No great cause can go far without pausing to energize. If the Kingdom of God is sometimes lax in what it ought to do, it may be that members of the church have not taken the time necessary to work and to pray."

Dr. Galloway had glowing words for his successor, Dr. Finis Crutchfield, and told his congregation, "I have asked him to ease up just a little and let me be missed at least three weeks." He served the San Antonio-Northwest Texas Area for four years, then returned to Arkansas to serve the Little Rock and North Arkansas conference for four years, and then the Southwest conference for fourteen years.

Paul Galloway retired in 1972, and moved immediately from Little Rock to Tulsa. He was given an office on the seventh floor of the tower at Boston Avenue, which he thoroughly enjoyed. But his work was not yet done. He was recalled at the death of Bishop Copeland in 1973 to serve the Houston area until 1976, and in 1983 he was recalled an unprecedented second time to fill the vacancy of the Bishop of Louisiana. Bishop and Elizabeth Galloway returned to Tulsa in 1984 to be active members of Boston Avenue. He died on August 4, 1990.

The Church Expands
Dr. Finis A. Crutchfield - 1960-1972

" | chose the ministry as an act of obedience. It was not mine to
consider whether I was especially suited, or whether the ministry
offered possibilities for personal advancement. I did not seek to
evaluate the role of the church or its ministerial office. The decision
was a matter of obedience."

The words are those of Dr. Finis Alonzo Crutchfield, a third-
generation clergyman, in a pamphlet on Christian vocations.

"I feel the Lord asks me to do this and it is not mine to know
why or fully to comprehend. Undoubtedly home training was a large
factor in the decision, yet the final choice was made somewhat apart
from this. When the Lord asks a person to make known His gospel
through preaching and living His Word, he must say yes or no.

"I have found the ministry to be immensely satisfying and
challenging because it deals with life's ultimate questions and final
answers; it places one amid people's daily lives where the great
dialogues of life are spoken; it exposes one's soul to the mysteries of
God's grace. But I chose to enter this field because I had to say yes or
no to Him."

Those words, and the fact that he was nominated for bishop
four times—three times voluntarily stepping aside—paint a clear
picture of the man who would serve Boston Avenue Church for
almost twelve years.

Born in Henrietta, Texas, in 1916, he married Benja Lee (Bennie)
Bell in 1941. They had one son, Charles, who would himself become
a Methodist minister. Bennie had grown up in the congregation of
Finis Crutchfield Sr., in Dallas, but paid little attention to his son. She
went to SMU while he was getting a degree from Duke University,
and they got reacquainted when both were active in youth work at
assemblies and conferences. They married when he was associate
pastor at First Methodist in Oklahoma City.

Crutchfield earned a BA from Southern Methodist University,
where he was president of the student body, and a Masters of
Divinity degree from Duke Divinity School. He was later awarded a
Doctor of Divinity degree from Oklahoma City University and a
doctorate in literature from the University of Tulsa.

After serving as assistant pastor at First Methodist in Oklahoma City, he was the pastor at Goodwell and Elk City, then at First United Methodist in Muskogee, and finally, he spent ten years at McFarlin Memorial Methodist Church in Norman, Oklahoma.

During his three years at Goodwell, he taught Shakespeare and English literature at Panhandle A & M College. A Greek scholar, he was known later to preach from Greek notes. A Goodwell member later recalled, "We knew we had somebody special after he had preached one sermon." Dr. Crutchfield was extremely popular with young people, and drew students by the hundreds in Goodwell, Norman, and Tulsa.

Dr. Crutchfield was only five feet and five inches tall. When he first came to Boston Avenue he stood on a wooden box at the pulpit to preach. Later the pulpit was lowered for him.

WILLARD STONE
WORLD-FAMOUS WOOD SCULPTOR WILLARD STONE WAS AN EXHIBITOR IN THE FIRST RELIGIOUS ARTS FESTIVAL.

During Dr. Crutchfield's tenure, an 8:30 a.m. Sunday worship service was instituted at Boston Avenue. It was also Dr. Crutchfield who began the tradition of wearing of robes in the pulpit of Boston Avenue Church, which is intended to focus attention on the function of the person in the service rather than on the individual. The worship experience was very important to Dr. Crutchfield, and he strongly encouraged worshippers to "Enter in quietness, wait in prayer, worship in reverence."

"Sometimes I think the Lord intended me to preach short sermons for I don't have much of a voice. And I'm not a good singer, either," he said. But he had many other gifts. He was a man full of energy, ideas, and enthusiasms. He helped establish numerous programs and classes during his years at the church.

In 1960, The Roundtable class was established under the guidance of the Reverend Ed Upton, Minister of Education. It was for young married couples who were interested in a discussion class, and the sponsors were Ed and Marjorie Monnet, Bill and Dot Blew, and Ivan and Shirley Griffith.

MRS. L. S. BARTON

FRED ELDER
THE ORGANIST OF BOSTON AVENUE
IS DRESSED FOR A CONCERT.

Boston Avenue Church's first Religious Arts Festival was held in 1961, drawing thousands of visitors and almost four hundred entries. It included not only visual arts such as adult and children's paintings and sculpture, but also encompassed drama, poetry, and music. Two artists represented there would become internationally famous in a few short years. Locust Grove artist Willard Stone submitted a wood sculpture called "Mary and the Christ Child." A stunning painting of a crown of thorns entitled "Easter Bonnet" was painted by Charles Banks Wilson. Wilson would become something of a "painter laureate" for the state of Oklahoma, for his portraits of major Oklahoma historic figures are featured in the rotunda of the state capitol, the Will Rogers Museum, and other public gathering places.

The Religious Arts Festival, chaired by Mrs. Norman Brown that first year, was designed as an opportunity for people to express their deepest feelings in art, poetry, or music. It would be an event celebrated each February for the next twelve years.

Dr. Hugh Perry became chairman of the board of stewards in 1961. An indication of how important missions had become at Boston Avenue by 1961 was that Hugh Perry also served on the Methodist general board of missions, one of only fifty laymen throughout Methodism on the missions board.

In 1962, Mrs. Barton established a lectureship fund in the memory of Dr. Louis S. Barton, Boston Avenue pastor from 1914 to 1922, who had died in 1953. Dr. Crutchfield said, "The gift from Mrs. Barton is of such a sum that we can attract the finest speakers in the world." This promise was fulfilled as the Barton lectures became a major annual event in the life of the church.

That same year, Sue and Dr. Duane Brothers, members of the Mr. and Mrs. class, worked several weeks in a hospital in Bolivia. This was the first of many such medical mission trips to Bolivia, Mexico, Haiti, and other countries. Organized, supplied, staffed, and underwritten by Boston Avenue members, these trips have brought a Christian witness in the form of medical, dental, and eye care to people in remote regions where such services are normally unavailable. At the same time, Boston Avenue's doctors, dentists, pharmacists, and assistants who have served as medical missionaries, have brought back a deeper understanding of developing countries, where conditions resemble those in which Dr. Brewer, Dr. Clinton, and Dr. Wilson practiced the healing arts during our city's pioneering days.

Through the years Duane Brothers, an anesthesiologist, has served on the Commission on Missions and Education and as superintendent of the youth department. In 1984, Sue Brothers would be a nominee for Tulsa Volunteer of the Year. "We could write a whole book on the Brothers' activities in mission work," commented Mary Metzel. "They have greatly broadened our understanding."

A class for people who are hearing impaired was established in 1962. Called Ephphatha class, it began with seventeen members. The Heritage class for young couples also was formed that year.

Fred Elder became the church organist in 1964. He held both bachelors and masters of music degrees from Westminster Choir College in Princeton, New Jersey. Fred would become known as one of the most outstanding church organists in the United States, serving in some of the highest offices in music associations throughout the country. He succeeded Barbara Benefiel, who moved to Alva to teach at Northwestern State University. She returned to Boston Avenue in 1972, when she became Mrs. Fred Elder.

While Dr. Crutchfield was pastor in Tulsa, the church completed a five year program of remodeling and construction. By 1960 the building was thirty-two years old, and the congregation it served had grown from less than two thousand to well over six thousand. More space was needed, updating was needed, and there were still parts of the original 1928 structure—such as the interior of the tower—that had never been finished, even though the building had been out of debt since 1946. The building committee, charged

SUE BROTHERS
A FAVORITE TEACHER, SUE BROTHERS HAS TAUGHT MANY CLASSES AT THE CHURCH THROUGH THE YEARS.

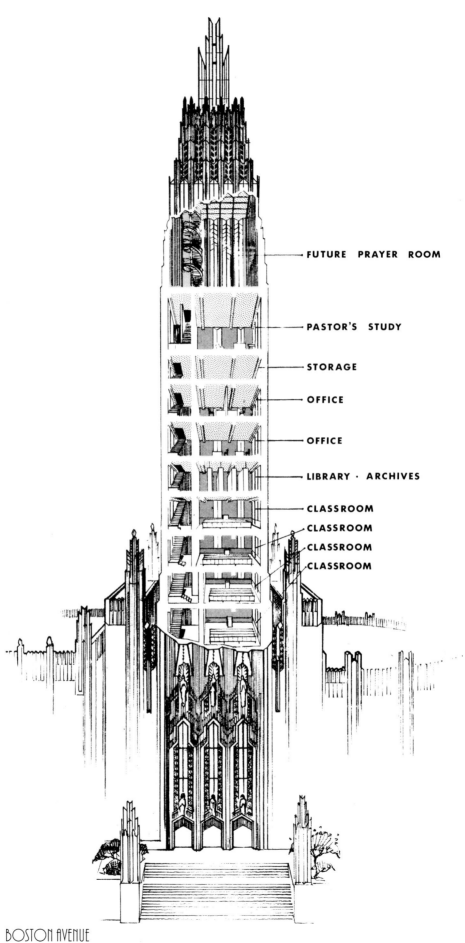

FUTURE PRAYER ROOM

PASTOR'S STUDY

STORAGE

OFFICE

OFFICE

LIBRARY · ARCHIVES

CLASSROOM

CLASSROOM

CLASSROOM

CLASSROOM

BOSTON AVENUE
UNITED METHODIST
CHURCH
150

**STRUCTURAL MODEL OF THE
BOSTON AVENUE CHURCH.**
THIS MODEL WAS DEVELOPED TO
ILLUSTRATE HOW THE EDUCATION
BUILDING WOULD BLEND WITH THE
ARCHITECTURE OF THE ORIGINAL
STRUCTURE. THE TOWER
RENOVATION PLANS WERE SET FORTH
IN THE DRAWING ON THE FACING
PAGE.

with carrying out the five-year program, was made up of Bob Bradshaw, H.G. Barnard, William L. Butler, Wright Canfield, Dr. A.B. Carney, George Cathey, L.C. Clark, Howard E. Felt, Clarence Glasgow, Theo. F. Hansen, Walter Helmerich III, Dan P. Holmes, Nathan Janco, E.C. Leonard, Jr., Mrs. W.A. Showman, Dr. Hugh Perry, Sr., and Mrs. Hugh Perry, Sr.

In 1960, the firm of McCune and McCune and Associates, Architects, A.I.A., presented a master plan for renovation, remodeling, and new construction. The plan included the addition of an educational building (or "children's" building); renovation of the sanctuary; refinishing of the chapel; remodeling of the second-floor offices; construction of new offices, work rooms, and classrooms in the tower; installation of an archives room; elevators; remodeling and redecorating of the third and fourth floors; and additional parking.

All projects were carefully planned and designed to harmonize with the original structure and follow the original symbolism of the church.

The main auditorium was closed for months in 1961 and church services were held at Central High School while a mosaic was installed on the wall behind the pulpit and choir loft. A mosaic had been part of the original 1920s plans for the sanctuary but had never

THE SANCTUARY

THE MOSAIC AND THE CROSS WERE ADDED TO THE SANCTUARY IN THE RENOVATION PROJECTS OF THE 1960s. BELOW IS THE SANCTUARY SKYLIGHT.

been designed due to a lack of funds. The 42' x 42' work was created by Italian artist Andrea Raffo. Its tiles were fabricated in Italy in the Raffo studio and laid out on the floor there. Art Johnson traveled to Italy to examine the work carefully. Once it passed his approval, each piece was numbered and the mosaic was shipped to Tulsa in small sections. Here, while all the seats were out of the sanctuary being refurbished, the mosaic was applied piece by piece to the wall.

Once the altar mosaic was installed, it made a stunning difference in the appearance of the sanctuary. The thousands of tiny tiles picked up the colors and light from the stained-glass windows, intensifying the beauty of the auditorium. Shading from white to dusty purple through the rose spectrum, the mosaic repeats the color and symbolism of the windows, with downstreaming lines to represent the light of God's grace, upward-reaching stalks of tritoma flowers, and radiating circles of coreopsis.

After the mosaic was in place, a thirteen-foot bronze cross was hung in the center where a circle is formed by the tiles. The hand-wrought cross was created by Duane Hatchett and is an empty cross but not a crucifix. Instead, it symbolizes the resurrection of Christ with a shape which carries the impression of a figure, once there, now gone.

A seventy-two-rank Moller organ, created in Hagerstown, Maryland, and considered one of the finest in the region, was installed during the 1961 remodeling of the sanctuary. Almost twice the size of the former sanctuary organ, it has four manuals (keyboards), exclusive of the foot pedals, and 4,174 pipes which were housed in the four chambers to the south and north of the choir loft and over the balcony. The organ installation was completed while Dr.

MAKING WAY FOR THE EDUCATION WING
HOUSES TO THE EAST OF THE CHURCH WERE REMOVED TO MAKE ROOM FOR THE EXPANSION THAT CREATED THE EDUCATION WING.

BOSTON AVENUE
UNITED METHODIST
CHURCH
154

Crutchfield was in India and he wouldn't allow organist Barbara Benefiel to play it publicly before his return two weeks later.

In 1965, the educational wing was added, the parking lot was expanded, and major renovations made to several areas. The addition of the educational wing enclosed the porte cochere and created a soaring room which became Bishops Hall. Members of the church would later enjoy this space particularly in the season before Christmas when a large wreath is hung from the ceiling and it is the scene of glorious music and the candlelighting festivities of Advent. The cantilevered structure also allowed members of the church who hadn't wanted to give up the porte cochere to be accommodated by a drive underneath the new building. Entrances were then provided on the lower level.

One of those to work on the church renovations was Murray McCune, a young architect in his family's firm, and a member of the church. According to Doc Metzel, McCune usually was told what the church wanted and worked hard to develop a design to accommodate it. When the education wing was being planned, Murray's question was, "How do you add to a perfect structure without destroying the symmetry?"

One afternoon, he and his brother were studying the structure and taking photographs of different angles. As the day grew later, a shadow cast by the tower lengthened across the building lot. Suddenly Murray called to his brother, "That's it! Get a picture of that shadow. That will be my building." And so it was.

Many of the materials used in the original structure — such as limestone and terra cotta — had become so expensive that their use in the new building was impractical. Terra cotta was by now almost a lost art. The limestone, with its many colors, was difficult even to imitate in affordable materials. For the new building, the architects suggested the use of a cast material matching the original terra cotta. This modern material would allow freedom in form but still provide economy in construction. Precast panels were designed, patterned from the features of the existing building.

A scaled-down version of the tower's glass and black metal fretwork appears at each corner of the new wing, echoing the dominant feature of the original building to provide a strong link between old and new. This corner treatment also provides light to the corridors in the new building, and gives the building an open

Two Generations Wed in the Rose Chapel

John and Martha Jo Bradley come down the aisle, left, after their wedding on August 30, 1941. At right, Patricia Bradley, daughter of John and Martha Jo, wore her mother's wedding dress when she married Rick Rose on August 31, 1968.

appearance inside and out. Just as envisioned by its architects, the new building falls within the shadow cast by the original building and tower in late afternoon.

The educational building was completed at a cost of one million dollars and opened in September, 1965. Soon after its construction it was awarded a top prize, the Regional Design Award, by the American Institute of Architects. The new building was at one time the largest two-way cantilevered structure in the United States.

Thirteenth Place south of the church was closed and numerous lots for parking were purchased, bringing the total spaces to four hundred. The new parking areas with their wide walkways incorporated planting segments and lighting designed to carry out the original themes of the 1928 structure. The cement used in the parking lot decorations was treated to match the material of the new education building.

By the mid-1960s, even with the new education building, the unfinished tower space was needed. Mr. and Mrs. L.C. Clark donated an elevator for the north foyer to serve the tower, and the space was finished into offices and meeting rooms. One of the first groups to make use of the tower was a new young couples class, established by Sharon and Lee Butler and Mary and Don Swalander in 1967. The Pilgrimage class met on the seventh floor of the tower from then until 1972.

A tower prayer chapel was finished in 1966 and consecrated in February, 1967. Occupying the top two floors of the tower, it was designed by H.G. Barnard, Jr., whose father had served on the building committee for original church structure in 1928. Stairs from the fourteenth floor lead to a fourteen-feet-square room, with a wood pillar in the center which forms the backdrop for an alter. Eight bench alcoves and eight window alcoves, including one in each of the four corners, jut out from the room, giving it a circular feeling. Overhead, steel crossbeams covered in wood support a sixteen-sided ceiling canopy which unfolds from a peak about fifteen feet above the alter at the center beam. A small cross on the alter is patterned after the sanctuary cross.

Furnishings and appointments for the chapel were acquired through gifts and memorials. Women in the church made needlepoint prayer cushions. Construction of the chapel was funded through donations by several generous members of the congregation.

It has long been a tradition at Boston Avenue Church that major contributions to the church are not recognized by naming the room or item after the donor. Thus, the tower chapel is not named for Mr. and Mrs. Horace G. Barnard, Sr., Mrs. Frederick P. Walter, Mrs. James A. Chapman and the late James A. Chapman's gift honoring Mr. and Mrs. Robert M. McFarlin. The carillon is not named for its donors, Mr. and Mrs. Armon Bost, and gifts by Mrs. W.K. Warren and her family (including the centennial mosaics in the Great Hall), Joe Holliman, or the Helmerichs are not named for them. The tower elevator does not bear the L.C. Clarks' names, and other significant additions to the beauty or utility of the church go similarly unnamed. It is a tribute to the generosity of the members of the church that they have not sought recognition for their gifts, large or small, but continue to give to assure that the church has what it needs to enhance its beauty and ability to serve the needs of its people.

In all, during the twelve years Dr. Crutchfield served the church, $7.5 million was expended on improvements to the physical

THESPIAN TALENT

ABOVE, THE CHURCH STAFF. WHAT A GROUP!

BELOW, THE REVEREND CHENOWETH (RAY LEWANDOWSKI) AND MRS. CHENOWETH (JO BETH HARRIS) IN THE 1968 RELIGIOUS ARTS FESTIVAL PRODUCTION OF "FOREVER BEGINNING."

plant, all of it paid for through donations.

Dr. Crutchfield earned many honors, both during his tenure at Boston Avenue and later. He was awarded the Brotherhood Award by the National Council of Christians and Jews in Tulsa for his work with prisoners at McAlester State Penitentiary. He would be praised for the brilliance of his mind, his motivation of action, the great visions and tremendous vitality which he possessed, and the spirit of evangelism with which he served the church. "He was the first Oklahoma pastor to show what inclusiveness means," one person said.

It was during Dr. Crutchfield's tenure at Boston Avenue in 1966 that the first Office of Indian Opportunity was housed at the church. Dr. Crutchfield gave the funeral message for Joe Hawkins, Boston Avenue's long-time, much-beloved custodian. This was the first funeral for a black person to be held in the church. Joe, who prepared coffee for every event held in the church for many years, had frequently commented that this was the "eatin'est" church he had ever seen.

As people began to be aware of the significance of the history of Boston Avenue Church, the need for church archives became apparent. The historical committee was appointed to help develop the archives, headed by John Eagleton. Establishment of the archives in 1965 coincided with the two hundredth anniversary of the first Methodist sermon preached in this country.

Several items belonging to the Reverend and Mrs. Chenoweth, the founding pastor and his wife, were donated by Margaret Chenoweth, their oldest daughter, who also shared information about her family and the early days of the church. Dr. Fred Clinton, who had written early members and pastors for information and had authored several books on early Tulsa, was responsible for much of what is known about the early history.

Ruby Mae Jones was named archivist. She had come to Tulsa in 1917, attended the University of Tulsa and earned a masters degree at OU, and taught English in Tulsa Public Schools for forty-three years. She was a founding member of the Tulsa County Historical Society and active in Friends of the Public Library.

Mary Metzel followed Ruby Mae Jones as archivist in 1968, and Martha Jo and John Bradley would take up the job in the mid-1980s. Mary and George (better known as "Doc") Metzel were vital to the growth of the church. Mary held some of the highest offices within the church organization ever achieved by a Boston Avenue woman. She would hold almost every office in the United Methodist Women, including president of the Oklahoma Conference. In 1969 she was a lay member of the Oklahoma Annual Conference. Later she would serve as a delegate to the general and jurisdictional conferences several times, a member of the General Council on

MARY METZEL

Finance and Administration for eight years, and as its president in 1980.

She and George would be honored in 1975 for twenty-seven years of faithful service in the Wesley Fellowship class, of which George was a teacher. Registrar at the University of Tulsa for thirty-two years, "Doc" would also be honored by that institution as "Mr. Homecoming" in 1976.

In 1967, John and Joanne Colbert were married by Dr. Crutchfield. She was an organist and he sang in the church choir. That was also the year of Murray Dickson's tragic death. Dr. James Alley, a specialist in public health, was selected to replace him as the church's missionary in Bolivia.

The Religious Arts Festival in 1967 featured portraits by photographer Bob McCormack of Boston Avenue members as the twelve disciples of Christ. McCormack volunteered to be the model for Judas. The others were: Ralph Morgan, James; Richard Cleverdon, Thaddaeus; Cecil G. Tyree, Bartholomew; William L. Butler, Matthew; Wallace O. Wozencraft, John; John Peterson, Peter; Charles M. Christensen, Phillip; Melvin C. Coiner, Andrew; Edward O Monnet, Thomas; Kenneth Robertson, James the Lesser; and Dr. Duane Brothers, Simon.

In 1968, a play called "Forever Beginning," depicting the beginning of the church and the days of the Chenoweth ministry was a feature of the Religious Arts Festival. Annawyn Shamas wrote the script and directed the play and Beth (Mrs. E.C.) Leonard was assistant director. W.I. (Nick) Nichols did the staging and lighting for the production and said, "It was one of the most pleasant and rewarding experiences I have ever had." "Forever Beginning" would be performed again in 1993 under the direction of Sylvia Tuers, to celebrate the church's centennial year.

Nick Nichols was a mainstay in the church for many years, lending his technical expertise to almost every church production held. An extremely talented actor, his patriotic rendition of "The Old Man and the Flag" was guaranteed not to leave a dry eye in the house. It also earned him a medal from the Freedom Foundation of Valley Forge, which was awarded to people deemed by the foundation to be great Americans. Nick's wife, Mary Nichols, was active in the Wesleyan Service Guild and other church activities, as well as serving the Tulsa Public Schools for thirty-five years as supervisor of music. After her death, the Republican Women named a women's club for her, in honor of her political work.

In 1968 the congregation celebrated its seventy-fifth

anniversary. Joe Hollimon, an attorney, chaired the diamond anniversary celebration committee. Hollimon also was a strong supporter of the Salvation Army in Tulsa, serving as board chairman for three years. As part of the anniversary commemoration, a portrait of Dr. Adah Robinson was donated to the church by Mrs. Frank Parsley.

The Methodist Church and the Evangelical United Brethren were united in 1968, and the resulting new denomination brought about the fifth name change for this congregation in its seventy-five year history. It now became Boston Avenue United Methodist Church. Boards and agencies throughout the churches were reorganized and renamed as well. For instance, the Woman's Society of Christian Service became the Women's Society of Christian Service.

Roger Cole Coffey and Cookie Guiou were married by the Reverend John Reskovac in 1970 in the church. Roger had been a lifelong member of Boston Avenue, but his name couldn't be found on the church rolls. He had changed it from Harold Roger Coffey, because he was the last male in the Cole family. Like his grandparents, the C.C. Coles, and his mother and aunts, Roger and Cookie Coffey would bring up their children in the church.

In 1972 an organ designed by Boston Avenue organist Fred Elder for the Rose Chapel and built by M.P. Moller, Inc., was donated by Mrs. H.G. Barnard in memory of her husband Horace Greeley Barnard. Among the many ways in which Mr. Barnard had served the church was as a member of the building committee for the Thirteenth and Boston building, as well as a member of the board of stewards.

DR. AND MRS. FINIS CRUTCHFIELD

When Dr. Crutchfield was elected bishop in 1972, his congregation, which numbered 6,800, was sad to lose him, yet proud of him. In his final appearance before the church board, he said, "A shepherd is judged by the quality of the wool on his flock. It is the quality of the people in this congregation which has made me effective."

During the eight years he served as Houston Area Bishop, 1976 to 1984, United Methodist membership increased 28,000 while most denominations were declining. The Chapel of Transfiguration at Camp Egan was given by Mr. and Mrs. Jim Egan, "to the glory of God and in appreciation of Bishop and Mrs. Finis Crutchfield and family who are friends and comrades in Christ of long standing."

In 1982, Bishop Crutchfield was named president of the United Methodist Church Council of Bishops, the highest office for a clergyman in the denomination. He retired in 1984, and died in 1987.

CHAPTER 16

New Ministries

DR. J. CHESS LOVERN - 1972-1976

As a poor farm boy in Georgia, the church was the only institution that claimed me with genuine acceptance and love," Dr. J. Chess Lovern said when he came to Boston Avenue in 1972. He was born in 1910 in Monroe, Georgia. "The pastors of my country church were the most friendly and attractive persons, beyond my home, who touched my life."

He attended Emory University in Atlanta for two years before transferring to Southern Methodist University on a football scholarship. After graduation, he completed Perkins School of Theology and received a Doctorate of Divinity from Southwestern University in Georgetown, Texas, and a second one from Oklahoma City University. He was married to Faye Pressley; they had a daughter, Lindy, and a son, Mark.

Dr. Lovern served ten years in the First Methodist Church in Lubbock, Texas, and five years at Laurel Heights Methodist Church in San Antonio, Texas. In a brochure for the Oklahoma Conference Commission on Christian Vocations he would later write, "My call to the ministry comes from God, through the attractiveness of the ministers I knew and the thrill of being accepted as a person by the church. My conviction is still that God wants us to lay His hands upon the life of the youth of today, through the attractiveness of the church and the winsomeness of those already in the ministry."

At the age of sixty-one, Dr. Lovern came to Boston Avenue after serving eight years at St. Lukes United Methodist Church in Oklahoma City. Although Tulsa and Oklahoma City were far larger than most towns he had served, he commented, "Our experience has been that people are about alike regardless of where they live or what they do."

In 1973 he wrote, "So many things are calling to us for attention in the church. We must not attempt any of them without the leadership of the Holy Spirit."

Boston Avenue Church lost a man who had become almost an institution when Marvin Reecher resigned in 1972. Reecher had built the church music program into one of the largest in the country over a span of thirty-two years. When he came to Boston Avenue in 1940,

DR. J. CHESS LOVERN

there were two choirs, one junior and one adult. When he left, there were fourteen music groups that involved more than six hundred members of the congregation. E.C. Leonard, chairman of the administrative board, honored Reecher's long service to the church, and Dr. Lovern expressed his personal thanks for Reecher's years of outstanding service.

Tom Clark, director of Edison High School's choral music program came to direct the Chancel and senior high choirs, and Bill Belen from California took over the junior high and junior girls' and boys' choirs. Larry Dean became director of music in 1973, a post he would hold until 1989.

The beautiful Christmas Eve service at Boston Avenue was made even more memorable by the addition of a tableau that accompanied the reading of scripture surrounding Christ's birth. An artifact of the church's founding years became part of the annual tableau: the cradle used by the church's first preacher and his wife for their infant son when they moved to Oklahoma in 1893, donated by Margaret Chenoweth, became Jesus' manger.

In August of 1973, Dr. Lovern suffered a heart attack, and was out of the pulpit for eight weeks. In a letter to the congregation following his recovery, he said, "thank you for building a bridge of love for us during 1973." Members of the congregation sent scores of cards and notes during his illness—many, no doubt prompted by the thoughtful notes he had written them. Dr. Lovern would be remembered for his letters and notes long after he ended his four years at Boston Avenue.

During his absence, there were several changes in the assistant pastoral staff. The Reverend Bob Dotson left to join Centenary Church in Tulsa and he was replaced as minister of education by the Reverend Harold Reynolds from Highland Park Methodist in Dallas. The Reverend Gordon Spencer replaced Lawrence Culbertson who left to attend Duke Divinity School in Durham, North Carolina. Charles H. Richardson also was on the staff, and Fred Elder was interim music director. These dedicated people filled in for Dr. Lovern until he was able to return to the Boston Avenue pulpit. It was a staff of unusual talent, devotion, and Christian dedication, he would later say.

TALENT AND DEVOTION
PICTURED, FROM TOP TO BOTTOM, ARE MARVIN E. REECHER AND LARRY DEAN, WHO GUIDED THE MUSIC PROGRAM, AND REV. GORDON SPENCER, BOSTON AVENUE'S WISE COUNSELOR.

The School for Continuing Education was begun by the Reverend Harold Reynolds shortly after he came here, and has

provided an outstanding variety of education programs through the years. N.B. Ingram was chairman of the steering committee for the first school. He was married to Melba Ingram, who had been president of WSCS from 1963 to 1965. Both served the church for many years.

The continuing education program was one of the ways in which Boston Avenue Church reached out to meet community needs, in keeping with Dr. Lovern's vision of what a large downtown church should be. "Downtown churches stand as a symbol and are a voice speaking for all churches," he said. Indeed, as the Crutchfield years at Boston Avenue had been characterized by building and renovation, the Lovern years were characterized by new ministries to the community.

Programs were developed at the church to meet many specific needs. Children's Day Out, a preschool for three and four year olds, was begun, headed by Lillian Hanson. Lillian had come to Boston Avenue in 1967 to help her friend Alice Wilder with the Mother's Day Out program, a drop-in babysitting service. "Alice and I had done Boy Scouts together, and I just came as a favor to help her out." Two years later Alice had left and Lillian became head of the program.

The change from Mothers' Day Out to Children's Day Out was more than just a name change. "We wanted to have a commitment from parents that their children would be there each time so we could plan programs for them." Twenty-six years after she came "just to help out" Lillian Hanson would still be at Boston Avenue, ably administrating Children's Day Out and all the church's programs for infants, toddlers, and preschoolers.

During Dr. Lovern's years at the church, many other special ministeries were begun as well. There were workshops for the public on topics related to problems such as stress, divorce, parental support, death and dying, cancer, marriage enrichment, and family life. Under Dr. Lovern's leadership, the Summer Venture program was begun, bringing college-age young adults to the church during the summer to work with children and youth. Special ministries for singles were begun during the Lovern years, and teaching ministries including Sunday evening Bible studies.

In 1975, the staff included the Reverend Art McGrew, the Reverend Thell Robertson, and the Reverend Jim Gragg. The Reverend Ray Menard coordinated development of a ministry to the deaf, establishing a deaf youth fellowship. Circle V would later be organized and Betty Powell would be hired in 1978 to be a staff advisor for the deaf ministry.

In 1976 Bob Bradshaw died while holding the office of chairman of the administrative board. He had served on the board for fifty years, and on the building committee for fifteen years. A bust of him was placed in the library with those of Dr. Rice, Dr. Robinson, and C.C. Cole.

A staunch supporter of the role of women in the church, in 1976 Dr. Lovern said "I'm amazed that the general conference is just becoming aware of the importance of women. I've known it all the time." After attending the Boston Avenue United Methodist Women's fall coffee, Dr. Lovern commented, "I've never been more impressed with a group of women. They reflect the many ways they serve the church, giving vitality and encouragement to me and to the other members of the staff."

He told the board of trustees at Oklahoma City University, which he served as chairman, "This is the day of 'Women's Lib,' but such a movement is not necessary in Boston Avenue. Our women are already serving with great distinction in all the organizational structure."

In addition to his leadership at Boston Avenue Dr. Lovern served for ten years as conference missionary secretary, was a member of the general conference committee to study episcopacy and district superintendency, and was involved in church posts

THE TOT LOT
PRESCHOOLERS PLAY OUTDOORS AT BOSTON AVENUE

throughout the region as well as civic organizations in Tulsa.

The Hall of Bishops was dedicated in 1975 in honor of Bishop Watts, Bishop Galloway, and Bishop Crutchfield, all former pastors of Boston Avenue. Dr. Lovern would take his own place in the Hall in 1976, when he became the fourth bishop elected from Boston Avenue. Once again, the congregation was both proud of their minister and chagrined to lose him. Bishop Paul Milhouse joked, "The people of Boston Avenue ought to be accustomed to it by now."

Dr. Lovern said, "For forty-one years as a Methodist pastor I have contended with bishops—silently, you understand. Now it is hard for me to believe I am one. If being a bishop provides half the satisfaction that we have received during these final days at Boston Avenue, it would be more than I could expect of the Good Lord."

When he left, he gave communion to the congregation, assisted by five associate pastors and John Russell, Tulsa district superintendent, who would become his successor at Boston Avenue. Bishop Lovern said, "You people are bishop-makers, even if you don't intend to be. Your devotion and concern have provided the vitamins on which I have lived."

Assigned to the South Central Jurisdictional Conference, he retired in 1980 and became Bishop in Residence and visiting professor at Texas Wesleyan College in Fort Worth. After his death in 1987, the Texas State Legislature unanimously passed a resolution in memory of J. Chess Lovern. It cited Bishop Lovern as "everybody's grandfather," and recalled his outstanding service to people and to the church. "This beloved clergyman will be remembered for his leadership, learned scholarship, and exemplary work as teacher, counselor, and pastor."

Constant Construction

Dr. John Russell - 1976-1980

W hen Dr. John Russell was named to succeed J. Chess Lovern in 1976, he didn't know he would be in the midst of a constant state of construction for the next few years. A Texas native, Dr. Russell was born into the family of a Methodist minister. He had earned a BA from Oklahoma City University, a Bachelor of Divinity degree from Perkins School of Theology, a Doctor of Divinity from Oklahoma City University, and did additional study at Phillips Graduate Seminary. He and his wife Mary Jean had three children, Debra Ann, Mary Margaret, and John Garrett.

He had served the First Methodist churches in Wagoner and Vinita, the Village United Methodist Church in Oklahoma City for four years, and First United Methodist Church in Enid for nine years. Mary Jean Russell, Dr. Russell's wife, was dearly loved by her young students as she directed children's choirs at Boston Avenue.

During the Russells' four-year tenure at Boston Avenue, there was constant construction. For one three-month period, Dr. Russell didn't even have an office. A "Tot Lot" was constructed just south of the education wing so that Boston Avenue children could safely play outside. Renovations to the building included replacement of boilers, installation of a new air conditioning system, remodeling of the multipurpose room, choir rooms, and bride's room among other projects.

Dr. Dan Brannin, an oral surgeon, chaired the board of trustees in 1976. Dr. Brannin also spearheaded a drive in Tulsa to end smoking in public places. He was succeeded by Armon H. Bost in 1977, the same year that Bost was inducted into the Oklahoma Business Administration Hall of Fame. Bost was a 1933 graduate of Oklahoma A&M (now OSU), from which his father had graduated in 1891. His mother was A&M's first woman graduate in 1896.

The Babies Milk Fund had became one

DR. JOHN RUSSELL

of Tulsa's most prominent charities. For several years, wrestling matches were held at the old Coliseum as one of its fundraisers. Boston Avenue matrons often teased each other about their enthusiastic cheering at ringside. The fund was ended in 1977 when it was determined that it was no longer needed, and the $4,600 left in the treasury was contributed to the Little Lighthouse.

Mae (Mrs. Walter) Thomas drew a crowd at Methodist Manor in April 1977 when she was honored by the commission on missions and the administrative board of Boston Avenue for her long years of outstanding service and participation in mission outreach for the church. Mrs. Thomas, 90 at the time, had chaired the mission fund to send Paul Mitchell as a missionary to Cuba in 1936 as a response to

REASONS TO CELEBRATE
TOP, MARY JEAN RUSSELL;
IMMEDIATELY ABOVE, I.V. GORDY
AND A CELEBRATION CAKE; RIGHT, A
CHURCH-SHAPED CAKE FOR THE
50TH BIRTHDAY OF THE THIRTEENTH
AND BOSTON BUILDING.

the challenge issued by the Reverend Forney Hutchinson. Since the church was heavily in debt at the time, all mission funds had to be raised separately.

Mrs. Thomas, who came to Tulsa in 1921, was also a life member of Hyechka and the WSCS, served on the Frances Willard Home board for twenty-five years, and was a member of the choir for forty years.

The Reverend Oral Roberts, founder of Oral Roberts University, preached both Sunday morning services at Boston Avenue on November 3, 1978. He and his wife joined Boston Avenue Church in 1968, leaving the Pentecostal Holiness Church after twenty-one years. Roberts studied to become a Methodist pastor and became a local elder in the Oklahoma United Methodist Conference.

Joe and Cathy Campbell helped establish the Seekers Sunday school class for couples in March 1978. They would still be active members fifteen years later.

LET THERE BE MUSIC
TOP, THINGS GET A LITTLE CRAZY AT SPRING SING TIME; BOTTOM, THE CHANCEL CHOIR, A LITTLE MORE INFORMAL IN REHEARSAL THAN IN PERFORMANCES.

A celebration that lasted several weeks commemorated the fiftieth anniversary of the Thirteenth and Boston building in 1979. The tritoma was adopted as the fifty-year celebration symbol, Martha Jo and John Bradley gathered up as many fifty-year members as possible to help celebrate, and Bishop Paul Galloway spoke at the third remembrance Sunday in May. On Celebration Sunday, June 10, a birthday cake was prepared for five hundred people, and Bishop Finis A. Crutchfield preached the sermon using Dr. John Rice's topic from June 9, 1929, "Ye Are My Witnesses."

George ("Doc") Metzel began a new series called "Fifty Years and Growing" for Sunday Night at Boston Avenue, and the church paper began a series written by Sheila Parr that reminisced about people and events fifty years before. I.V. Gordy celebrated fifty years of singing in the Chancel Choir, beginning when Belle Vickery

Matthews was directing.

"Spring Sing," an all-church song-fest begun by the Roundtable class in 1976, centered that year around songs from the 1929 era. With the talented Pete Stamper as master of ceremonies, people never knew exactly what to expect, but they knew it would be fun.

It was an appropriate year for the church to be named to the National Register of Historic Places "in recognition of the outstanding significance of this property." Mary Caroline Cole, who had done much of the application work toward achieving the recognition, presented the framed award to Mary Metzel for the archives.

By this time, Mary Caroline had made a few contributions of her own to the decor of the church which her parents had been so instrumental in building. In 1951 she designed the prayer rail for the Rose Chapel. Later as a member of the archives committee she designed display cabinets for the archives room.

Margaret (Mrs. Parke) Muir, was asked by Dr. Russell to head a new shepherd's program for the church. The program involved recruiting individuals and families in the church to be responsible for eight or ten people or families in their neighborhoods who were members of Boston Avenue Church. Through the personal contact and caring, the church could retain some of the better qualities of smaller churches in earlier times. Mrs. Muir had joined the church staff in 1970 as a church visitor, was a delegate to the Oklahoma Annual Conference for several years, and was a past president of the United Methodist Women.

Two great dreams of Dr. Russell's for Boston Avenue became reality during his tenure there. The first was an endowment fund for maintaining the building so that future funds donations to the church could go for programs. That dream came true when the special Charge Conference unanimously adopted a resolution creating a building maintenance endowment in 1979, one church member made an initial contribution of fifty thousand dollars, and others came forward to fund the endowment of two million dollars. These grants, gifts, and bequests would be held in trust, and their interest used to maintain the building. At the same time, Dr. Russell set a goal of two million dollars to be added to an endowment fund which was created in 1962, to be used at the discretion of the board.

His other great dream was to re-establish the church's television ministry, and the plans for that were approved toward the end of his pastorship. The Reverend Harold Reynolds and Johnnie Cherblanc were the key persons who implemented those plans. Johnnie Cherblanc was chairman of the church communication committee in 1978. He and his wife Judie were early members of the Roundtable class, and she was one of the hardest working and most organized members of church circles and the Frances Willard Home Auxiliary. Over the coming years Johnnie would give many hours of

PETE STAMPER, READY TO GO ON AS EMCEE OF THE 1983 SPRING SING.

MARGARET MUIR

valuable service in making possible the production of the church's television broadcasts.

The Bethel Bible Series began in January of 1979, with thirty-one persons starting the teacher training phase. Mildred Bolds Day was celebrated on February 18, 1979, as she retired after thirty-three years of service to the church. She had worked as secretary for Drs. Galloway, Crutchfield, Lovern and Russell, and said, "It was great. No two pastors were alike, and no one had the privilege of working for a finer group of men than I did."

Not all Sunday school classes have a creed, but the following beautiful one was adopted by the Finders class for singles when it was established in 1979:

We believe in the Holy Trinity, God the Father and Creator, Jesus Christ, His Son as our example, and the Holy Spirit; man created in the image of God; the unity of the fellowship of this class; the mercy of God and the forgiveness of sins; the need to understand each other and be supportive, even though we are different personalities brought together as one; supporting our church with our prayers, presence, gifts and service; and showing our faith by works and fellowship.

Some of the active members when the class became established were Jane Terhune, Judy Geiger, Bruce Combest, Rick Anderson, Clint Purtell, Nancy Porteus, and Whit Mauzy.

Construction of a different kind was underway in 1979, this time around the church. Construction of the expressway interchange partially encircling the church had begun. On March 16 the south parking lot was virtually inaccessible. "The Highway Department said they goofed," Dr. Russell reported. "They have promised it won't happen again." The Highway Department, however, drew words of praise from many church members for their cooperative attitude and careful attention to details that enhanced the church wherever possible, instead of detracting from it.

Part of the construction included a retaining wall between the expressway and the church parking lot. The church built a wrought iron fence atop the retaining wall which matched the planters near the doors.

In 1979 Roger Cole Coffey became chairman of the building committee, the same position his grandfather held when the

Thirteenth and Boston church was built, and a post he would continue to hold into the church's second century. "I grew up feeling like my family had a proprietary interest in the church building," Roger would later say. He had followed in his aunt Mary Caroline's footsteps to become an architect, and had opened his own firm in Tulsa in 1972.

"Mary Caroline Cole was my own personal Auntie Mame," Roger recalled. "She had a tree growing up through the middle of her house and a beautiful place she'd designed at the lake, and she'd call me to come over and hold the measuring tape for her when she was working on a project." She had never married and had children, but from the 1940s she always had an English bulldog. She drove a convertible, "with the top down, going ninety-nine miles an hour," he recalls, "with the bulldog in the back seat, its ears flapping in the breeze." Just as she had been influenced to become an architect by her parents' and Adah Robinson's work on the church building, Roger decided at age ten he wanted to be an architect like his exciting Aunt Tot.

In 1988 Mary Caroline Cole would be awarded the highest honor given an architect by the American Institute of Architects, the FAIA. This was in recognition of her years of work championing the cause of handicapped access to both public and private buildings. The church building at Thirteenth and Boston which had inspired her architectural career continued to gain acclaim as the years went by. It was named "America's Most Beautiful Art Deco Church," and in 1979 was featured in the book *Tulsa's Art Deco,* published by the Junior League of Tulsa.

In June 1979, C.C. (Mac) and Grace McCrary celebrated their sixtieth wedding anniversary. She had come to Tulsa from Chickasha in 1913 when the Reverend Percy Knickerbocker was pastor. She was in the last graduating class of Central High School when it was still located at Fourth and Boston. In 1916, the new school was opened on Sixth between Cincinnati and Detroit. Mac came to Tulsa that year, and Mac and Grace met in the Epworth League. Dr. Barton was the pastor at the time, and Mac was president of the Young Men's class taught by C.C. Cole. They

THE INTERDISPERSAL LOOP
CONSTRUCTION OF THE LOOP DRAMATICALLY CHANGED THE AREA SURROUNDING THE CHURCH.

BOSTON AVENUE
UNITED METHODIST
CHURCH
174

became engaged in June 1918 just before he left to serve in the U.S. Army in World War I, and they were married by the Reverend House in June 1919 when Mac returned. (Dr. Barton was still in Europe serving as a chaplain.)

Mac McCrary had served continuously on the administrative board since 1919, had been superintendent of the Sunday school, played on the baseball team, was scout master of Troop 20, and had been head offering bearer for seventeen years. Grace was just as active, being president of both the general society and board of the Women's Society, and was a charter member of Mrs. Rice's Mother's Club. She helped in the nursery and taught a girls' Sunday school class. They had three daughters, Peggy, Mary Lee and Maxine. Peggy had been baptized June 9, 1929, the Sunday of the official church dedication.

Service to the church and the community was something Grace had learned by example. Her mother, Kate Tuttle, was still doing telephoning for the Women's Society in 1973 just before she died at the age of 103. Kate was the daughter of General J.A. Yeager, a Tulsa pioneer and street commissioner under Mayor Wooten in the early 1900s. She grew up in a big white house at Fourth and Denver. In 1890, she was married to Claude Tuttle, a banker from Texas. She became a member of Boston Avenue in 1913, taught the Philathea class for young ladies and was a charter member and an honorary life member of WSCS.

During Dr. Russell's pastorate, he was not only active in the Oklahoma Conference, holding the chairmanship of significant committees, he also worked hard in the civic affairs of the community, as he had done wherever he had served. In Tulsa, he was particularly active in Tulsa Metropolitan Ministry and Goodwill Industries.

In July 1980, Dr. John Russell was elected a bishop. His son John Garrett Russell said, "I am so proud of my daddy." So was his congregation. Bishop Russell later was honored by Oklahoma City University as that school's first graduate to be elevated to the office of the Episcopacy in the United Methodist Church.

This was the fourth bishop elected from the Boston Avenue pulpit, and by 1980, the congregation was ready to trade its reputation as a "bishop-maker" for a senior minister it could keep around for a longer period of time.

FACING PAGE, DRAMATICALLY LIGHTED, THE CHURCH IS AS BEAUTIFUL AT NIGHT AS IT IS DURING THE DAY. ABOVE, C. C. (MAC) MCCRARY, 1919.

CHAPTER 18

LITURGY WITH ENERGY

DR. M. MOUZON BIGGS, JR. - SINCE 1980

arvin Mouzon Biggs, Jr., had never seen Boston Avenue
Church before being assigned here in 1980. His unusual
name has an illustrious history. He had been named for his
father, who had been named for two Methodist bishops.
Bishop Edwin Mouzon was the presiding officer of the Eastern
Oklahoma Conference of the Methodist Episcopal Church South
from 1915 to 1921. He gave strength and continuity to the rapidly
growing conference, helped establish Southern Methodist University,
and organized what would become the Perkins School of Theology.
Bishop Enoch M. Marvin (1823-1877) was said to have done the most
of any man to rouse Southern Methodism from defeatism after the
Civil War. He guaranteed five thousand dollars for Indian mission

DR. MOUZON BIGGS

work, raising the money by traveling to different conferences to tell the story, and supplementing it with his own funds.

In 1919, John Thomas Biggs and his wife, who were great admirers of Bishop Marvin, heard Bishop Mouzon preach in Marshall, Texas. They were so impressed that they named their son, born a few months later, Marvin Mouzon. The Biggses prayed that their son might become a great preacher. Instead, he became a great layman, and their grandson became a great preacher.

Marvin Mouzon Biggs, Jr., was born in Carthage, Texas, in 1941. Active in the Methodist church from childhood, he felt called to the ministry during a revival he attended as a teenager, and planned to attend Southern Methodist University after his high school graduation. Instead, the Methodist church assigned him to pastor two small country churches, the Mount Zion Circuit, in rural east Texas. At age eighteen, he attended college classes at Panola College in Panola, Texas, during the week, then prepared and preached two sermons every weekend at his churches.

BISHOP EDWIN D. MOUZON

Biggs received a Bachelor of Arts degree from Centenary College of Louisiana; a Master of Theology degree from SMU; and a Doctor of Divinity degree from Texas Wesleyan University in Fort Worth. He later received an honorary Doctor of Humane Letters degree from Oklahoma City University.

Dr. Biggs served as assistant pastor of Memorial Drive Methodist in Houston, Texas. After two years, he became associate pastor of First Methodist in Houston for seven years, four of those as administrative minister. From 1974 to 1980, he was pastor of Trinity United Methodist Church in Beaumont, Texas, where the church received more than two thousand new members during his pastorate.

He and his wife, Gayle Pedro Biggs, have a daughter, Allison, and two sons, Marvin Mouzon Biggs III (Trey), and Jason Paul Biggs.

When John Russell was elected bishop in 1980, Bishops Galloway and Crutchfield, both of whom knew Dr. Biggs, decided he was the right man to fill the pulpit at Boston Avenue Church. They recommended him to Bishop Milhouse, and in 1980 he was offered the post. Dr. Biggs recalls, "I said to Bishop Crutchfield, 'I've been a Texan all my life. What if they don't like me up there? I've never even been to Tulsa.' He assured me that the church in Tulsa loved its pastors, and 'has never fired one yet.' I had known and respected the last four pastors at Boston Avenue, and finally accepted the position."

When Dr. Biggs preached his first sermon in Tulsa, the congregation knew Boston Avenue had been blessed with a preacher of exceptional talent—blending intellect, wisdom, and warmth to bring a message that both educated and inspired worshippers. They would soon learn Dr. Biggs had a genius for administration as well. The church had 6,200 members when he came, and by 1991 had grown to 7,700.

REVEREND VIRGINIA GRAY
AND MARJORIE MONNET

Dr. Biggs downplayed his own contribution to this record, saying, "The church was really poised for growth. The Broken Arrow Expressway and interdispersal loop had recently been completed and the church parking lot was just being finished. The television ministry, approved while Dr. John Russell was pastor, also became a reality in March 1981, and has been a strong, positive influence for the church. It serves many homebound members of the church as well as countless others we don't know about.

"We had a good test of our television effectiveness when Channel Eight bumped us for the World Football League for three months in 1991," Dr. Biggs recalled. "Attendance stayed the same among our members, but the number of visitors began to decrease. Apparently, there were a number of letters to the station protesting our being pre-empted, and we were told it wouldn't happen again. Ironically, we drew more viewers than the World Football League!"

But television is far from the only way Boston Avenue Church reaches out into the community. A good example is the Barton lecture series, which became the Barton-Clinton lecture series in 1988. The lectures have become an attraction throughout the community for those who wish to hear outstanding speakers of national stature. The Barton lectures had been established in 1963 by Mrs. L.S. Barton in memory of her husband, Boston Avenue's former pastor. But after twenty-five years, a need had developed to increase the funding for the lectures. Mrs. Beulah Jane Clinton had left funds to establish a lectureship in memory of her husband, Dr. Fred S. Clinton, and both families agreed that the money should be combined to ensure the continuation of outstanding lectures. The Barton-Clinton lectures are a living memorial to two of Boston Avenue's finest men.

One of the most successful innovations during Dr. Biggs' pastorate has been the Old Time Revival in July each year. July was typically the lowest month for everything—attendance, Sunday school, and contributions. July 4 was the lowest Sunday of the year. In 1981, July became Old Time Revival month, with funeral home fans, favorite hymns, and a general feeling reminiscent of small town revivals. It has been so successful that July has become one of the peak months of the year.

The Rose Chapel was the scene of the wedding of Elizabeth Davis and Clifton Forrest in 1982. Elizabeth, the daughter of Dr. and Mrs. John Rice, had married Sterling Davis in the chapel in 1965, and had been widowed in 1980. She was an art teacher at Eliot Elementary for twenty-five years.

Broadway came to Boston Avenue in 1983 when a popular series of musicals was begun by Larry Dean, director of music, and church members Carl Sieberts and Sylvia Tuers. The productions involved large casts of church members of all ages who auditioned, rehearsed, and performed whole-heartedly through the coming years. Sylvia Tuers served as director for the first three musicals, *Brigadoon, Anything Goes,* and *Desert Song.* Then Johnnie Cherblanc, who had performed in the first three, took over the reins for *Meet Me in St. Louis* and *Hello Dolly.* The musicals have been eagerly looked forward to—and sold out—each summer.

The support of families throughout the years has been one of the main factors in the growth of the church. In many cases, several generations have contributed time, talent, and money to help the church achieve its goals.

Ed Monnet, a dedicated member of the church for many years, followed in his uncle Forrest Darrough's footsteps in becoming chairman of the administrative board in 1983. Marjorie, Ed's wife, along with teaching Sunday school, has served as an administrative board member and a regional interpreter for United Methodist curriculum. Their son Edward, who grew up in the church, serves as offering bearer and as a fourth grade Sunday school teacher—a unanimous favorite among

BROADWAY AT BOSTON AVENUE
IMMEDIATELY BELOW, BABA'S PRODUCTION OF *OKLAHOMA!* DREW SOME OF BOSTON AVENUE'S FINEST SINGERS. (THIS IS PROBABLY THE ONLY TIME BRICE VENABLE WILL EVER BE SEEN IN BIB OVERALLS!) BOTTOM, CHARACTERS FROM THE CAST OF BABA'S PRODUCTION OF *MEET ME IN ST. LOUIS* INCLUDED, LEFT TO RIGHT, CARL SIEBERTS, CONNIE MORRISON, PATTI GASSAWAY, AND KENT HARRIS.

children at Boston Avenue. Now, his sons are growing up in the church as well, the fourth generation of church membership for the Darrough/Monnet family.

Another fourth-generation member is John H. Bradley, son of John and Martha Jo Bradley, grandson of the H.H. Copples, and great-grandson of Mrs. J.H. Powell. John has served in such areas as homebound ministries and as head of the communion committee. The sons of Roger Cole Coffey and Cookie Coffey, who are the great-grandsons of Mr. and Mrs. C.C. Cole, took their places in the church as they began to grow up, singing in the choir and serving as acolytes.

Another of the church's steadfast families is the Helmerich family. W.H. Helmerich II, a native of Chicago, had married the former Cadijah Colcord in Oklahoma City in 1919 and co-founded Helmerich and Payne in 1920 as a contract drilling company. Moving to Tulsa in 1927, the firm would become a significant part of the city's oil industry, eventually branching out into real estate. W.H. Helmerich was inducted into the Oklahoma Hall of Fame in 1978, and his family had a bronze statue erected in his memory at Twenty-first and Utica called "The Newspaper Reader." The seated man is reading a newspaper dated December 18, 1981—the day W. H. Helmerich died.

He had been a member and supporter of Boston Avenue, and his son and daughter-in-law, Walter H. Helmerich III and Peggy Helmerich, have been steadfast in their continued support. Walt served as chairman of the executive committee for many years, and Peggy is a popular Sunday school teacher and a member of the Women's Society.

They also have been prominent in Tulsa, supporting projects that would benefit the community. The Helmerichs were major contributors to the drive to restore the Tulsa Garden Center, and have quietly supported dozens of worthy causes in the city through the years including the Hillcrest Medical Center Cancer Center. They were recipients of the Outstanding Philanthropist Award from the National Society of Fund Raising Executives in 1985, and Peggy was named a Press Club Headliner in 1987. The Helmerich Library at 5131 East Ninety-first Street was named for Peggy, a library commissioner and the largest single contributor to the Tulsa Library Trust.

Sheila and Royse Parr, early members of the Roundtable class, have been involved in many different aspects of church life since 1960. Royse, a lawyer, has served on several committees, including the grounds committee. Sheila, a church employee for a while, serves on the building committee and has been deeply involved with renovation and redecorating projects.

Ruby Galloway Farish, an active member of the congregation for more than thirty years, was selected over more than three hundred others to deliver the laity address to the 1992 General Conference of the United Methodist Church. The daughter of a circuit-riding Methodist minister in Arkansas, the Reverend Jess Galloway, she holds a degree in philosophic studies from Hendrix College in Arkansas. Ruby believes firmly in participation by members of the congregation. "The professional clergy cannot possibly do all that is needed in the world around us."

She puts her beliefs into practice, and her record of achievements in the church and the community is long and impressive. She was named Volunteer of the Year by the Community Service Council in 1988; taught an adult Sunday school class; served on the board of United Methodist Cooperative Ministries; helped start Parents Anonymous, and serves as a facilitator of Parent and Child Center of Tulsa, a county-sponsored organization which grew out of Parents Anonymous; she is a certified mediator for the Early Settlement program in municipal court, a listener in Resonance; and one of twelve volunteer chaplains for the Tulsa Police Department, to name just a few of her activities.

RUBY FARISH

Ruby had been taught, and she and her husband Joseph taught their children, "If God has called me to do something, God will equip me to do it." Their son, Dr. Kent Galloway Farish, followed in his father's footsteps to become a family practice physician in Tulsa. Both Farish daughters followed in their grandfather's footsteps and became Methodist ministers. The Reverend Jessica Farish Moffatt is an associate pastor at First Methodist Church in Tulsa, and the Reverend Karen Farish Miller is a member of the North Carolina Methodist Conference.

Another of Boston Avenue's many outstanding women, Nancy (Mrs. George) Foster, was elected president of the Tulsa district of the board of missions and church extension in 1987, and then President of the Oklahoma conference of United Methodist Women. Only one other president of the group (Mary Metzel) had come from Boston Avenue. Nancy had served on the board three years before becoming president, and in 1991 she became the first woman ever to be elected chairman of the church's administrative board.

Many programs have been initiated or have grown significantly during Dr. Biggs' pastorship. Respite Care, designed to provide a "time-out" for parents of children with handicaps, began when the Reverend Gordon Spencer recognized the need and worked with Dr. Biggs to establish it. A Parents of Murdered Children group was founded by Dr. Charles and Shari Farmer in 1984, to provide emotional support, help deal with the rights of victims' families, and to take action when necessary to right wrongs in the judicial system.

Sunday school classes were established as the needs developed. The New Directions class for single people in their twenties was formed in 1983. Steve and Kathy Bunting, Sue Ella Matthews, and Jim Bentz served as coordinators. A young couples class which Ruby Farish helped launch in 1985 was named the Young Disciples.

THE MARANATHA CLASS
THE MARANATHA CLASS WORKS ON A HOUSE THEY ADOPTED AS A PROJECT.

Sometimes, the work of Boston Avenue groups is recognized outside the church. The Maranatha class of young couples who believe in working for their community was nominated for Volunteer of the Year in Tulsa in 1985. The class had worked for three years on the winterization program sponsored by the Tulsa Metropolitan Ministry, helped support Parents Anonymous, Meals on Wheels, Volunteers in Mission and many other programs.

In 1987, a Homebound Ministries program for members not able to attend church, was begun by Thelma (Mrs. Harold) Reynolds, and the Reverend Art McGrew. By 1992, there were almost 250 on the "Insider" rolls being visited, helped, and loved by 145 volunteers, keeping them in touch with their church and the world. Emma Richardson, a former staff member returning to Boston Avenue, became the director in 1991.

The Volunteer in Mission program is a movement that encourages individuals and churches to do service projects for people and institutions in need. In 1983, the board of global ministries in Oklahoma became part of that program, and Boston Avenue has participated several times. In 1987, a home VIM team provided medical services to the Frances Willard Home. A medical team went to provide services in Jamaica in 1988, and a team went into the Cookson Hills in Oklahoma in 1991. Local missions receive attention, too. For instance, the church provided a place for a Chinese congregation to meet for two years.

"The growth of endowment funds has helped us underwrite growth for the future," Dr. Biggs reported. The Boston Avenue church endowment fund and the maintenance endowment funds today total more than six million

VOLUNTEERS IN MISSION
TOP AND CENTER, VIM TEAMS RETURN HOME TIRED BUT HAPPY. BOTTOM, VOLUNTEERS WORK AT FRANCES WILLARD HOME.

dollars, and generate over $400,000 each year for maintenance and expansion. The building maintenance endowment fund was established in 1962, with the income dedicated solely to maintenance of the building and property. A general endowment fund was added later, with the income to be spent on whatever projects the finance committee and board agree are needed. A mission endowment fund was established, with the income dedicated to missions, and a native American endowment fund was established to be spent on projects for native Americans.

The building maintenance endowment fund has made it possible for the building at Thirteenth and Boston to remain a national historic treasure while serving the ongoing needs of a growing congregation. When the building was opened in 1927, Dr. John A. Rice wrote of it, "Without halting, it has gone forward to its present state of perfection but the end is not yet. There are several features that may not be worked out for years to come. We wanted evolution—creation through growth—to be the key idea."

With the help of the building endowment, this evolution continued through the 1980s and into the 1990s. A major program of systematic refurbishing and renovating was planned and began to be carried out step by step as funds became available. As it had been from the beginning, those involved in each project kept as their guiding philosophy the need to harmonize with the original structure, materials, and symbolism.

Projects included refinishing of the sanctuary organ, which enlarged it from seventy-two to 105 ranks. Over two thousand new pipes were added in the sanctuary. To enclose the organ pipe facades and incorporate them into the decor of the sanctuary, Roger Coffey designed wood casings which carry out the sanctuary's arched angle motifs.

RENOVATION

RENOVATION PROJECTS BEGINNING IN 1987 INCLUDED MAJOR WORK ON THE SANCTUARY.

Classrooms on the third and fourth floors were renovated in 1987 and on the first floor in 1990. In 1988, the small dining room was refurbished, the multi-purpose room remodeled and showers and a kitchenette added, and the bride's room enlarged, the walls mirrored, and new furnishings added.

The public, highly visible areas of Bishops Hall and the center hall received major attention. The

carpeting in Bishops Hall was replaced with terrazzo from the same quarry used in 1929, and the ceiling in the center hall elevated and pitched to repeat the angle theme. Furnishings, carpeting, and fabrics were selected for the center hall that carry the church's symbols. The information desk was remodeled, an entrance for those with physical limitations was upgraded, and the north hall was widened for a volunteers' desk and enclosed coat rack. A gallery was created for the display of photographs and archival collections.

A 1990 project centered around the Rose Chapel, parlor, kitchenette, and groom's room. Terrazzo was installed in the chapel and serving area of the parlor. The pews were modified for greater comfort, the communion rail redesigned, and the crosses highlighted. In the parlor, the ceiling was coffered and arched. Using the colors and motif of the rose windows as a guide, carpets, furniture, and paint were refurbished. The groom's room and kitchenette were relocated and expanded.

Scaffolding became a familiar sight in the sanctuary during 1991 and 1992 while the dome received twelve shades of descending color and replacement of gold leaf. At the same time, walls, woodwork, and stained glass were refurbished, and other enhancements added.

Community Hall was remodeled in 1992, receiving new tile, carpeting, enhancement of the serving windows and stage areas, and other improvements. An approved ramp for the physically limited replaced the old ramp. The music department received a major remodeling, including the large choir room, children's practice room, robe rooms, music library, and storage areas.

The progressive attitude, vision, and direct involvement of Dr. Biggs was a catalytic force throughout the planning and execution of each renovation. The building endowments ensured that funds were available for these projects.

Another major factor in these projects was the involvement of professionals in the fields of architecture and interior design who have given their time, talent and dedication without remuneration. As chairman of the building committee, Roger Cole Coffey, architect, A.I.A., lent his expertise and untold hours over more than fifteen years in helping to enhance and preserve the church which his grandparents had given so much to build; Jody Kaufman, A.S.I.D., coordinated a major part of the interior decorating; Lee Butler was responsible for a portion of the construction work; and Sheila Parr donated hundreds of hours, as well as her imagination and energy in keeping the projects moving in the right direction and providing coordination.

Growing at the rate of seven new members each Sunday, by 1991 the church had an urgent need for more parking. When the Fred Jones Ford dealership decided to move out of downtown that year, Boston Avenue had the opportunity to purchase enough land adjacent to the church to more than double the number of parking spaces. The purchase was made possible by major gifts from the Holliman and Warren families and many smaller contributions from other church members.

Part of the growth in church membership could be attributed to Dr. Biggs' abilities not only as a preacher and administrator, but as a Sunday school teacher as well. When he arrived at Boston Avenue in 1980, Dr. Biggs began teaching the Bible to adult Sunday school classes. He called it "a six-month run through the Bible," teaching a book of the Bible each Sunday. These series were so popular that in 1988 he began a verse-by-verse Bible study group in the Rose Chapel during the Sunday school hour. This class soon outgrew the chapel and moved into the sanctuary.

In 1989, Fred Elder succeeded Larry Dean as director of music, in addition to remaining the church organist. He was joined late that year by Casey Cantwell, who was named associate organist and associate director of music for the church.

A piece of Boston Avenue history came home in 1991, when the "Forgotten Angel" (as Mrs. James Gardner dubbed it during Dr. Crutchfield's pastorate) was returned to the church. It was a sculpture of an angel which had been left over from the construction of the building in 1928. Dr. Adah Robinson had suggested that Dr. Rice keep it in his garden at home, and there it stayed for more than sixty years. Returned to the church in 1991, it was left temporarily in the east parking lot, then stolen. An eastside Tulsan found it in his renter's garage and returned it to the church. Finally, it was placed in the courtyard of the educational building, to be surrounded by flowers and watched over by the sculptures of Robert Strawbridge and Phillip Embury.

The Strawbridge and Embury sculptures represent the building of the first Methodist churches in America. Strawbridge built a log chapel with his own hands that was one of the first meeting houses in America, and Embury built the first meeting house in New York City. Those sculptures had been on the east side of the building under the porte cochere, and were moved to the walls facing into the garden courtyard when the educational building was built and Bishops Hall created.

The church lost two of its best loved ministers in 1992 when the Reverend Art McGrew and the Reverend Harold Reynolds retired. Hospitalized church members had been strengthened and cheered for many years when Art McGrew's kind face appeared in their door. Harold Reynolds was an energetic, dedicated minister, who was very quick to spot needs which the church could meet and implement programs for that purpose.

In 1992, the world became aware of the starvation conditions in Russia, and Boston Avenue Church decided to participate in Food

REV. ART MCGREW

to Russia, a program coordinated by the Methodist Committee on Relief. Under the leadership of the Reverend Rodney Newman and Missions Chair Mark Butterworth, and working through Russian Orthodox Christian Priests, the project caught the imagination of the generous people of Boston Avenue. Expecting perhaps $1,000 in monetary contributions and some food to help in the effort, the organizers were stunned to receive sixteen thousand dollars and enough food to feed about five hundred families. Eighty members showed up to pack the supplies for shipping.

The Frances Willard Home celebrated its seventy-fifth birthday in 1992, and a campaign was begun to establish an endowment fund for it. The conference had taken over the responsibility for the home in 1958. Beverly Golden, Peggye Enlow, and Francis Willard Home Administrator Anna-Faye Rose were instrumental in the realization of the $750,000 goal.

By 1993, Dr. Biggs had served the church longer than any other pastor in Boston Avenue's history. He was named Tulsa's best spiritual leader by *Tulsa People* magazine in 1989, and

was honored in 1991 by the Tulsa Metropolitan Ministry for his interfaith work. He has also been active in issues regarding day care, including service on the day care licensing coalition.

Dr. Biggs has continued the custom of wearing robes in the Boston Avenue Church pulpit begun by Dr. Finis Crutchfield. Called John Wesley Robes, they resemble the robes worn by John Wesley at the time of the beginning of the Methodist Church. Dr. Biggs has added the wearing of the stole in the colors of the seasons of the Christian year, which are placed upon a minister at the time of ordination, and the yoke which symbolizes the bearing of his people's concerns to God and God's word to his people. Other portions of the service reflecting the church's Anglican roots that have been added include the processional with acolytes bearing the cross to the altar and lighting candles.

Dr. Biggs' spellbinding sermons follow a definite theme. His philosophy on sermons is a liturgical one. Instead of centering his preaching around a few favorite themes, he bases his sermons on the Revised Lectionary adopted by the United Methodist Church, preaching one year on Hebrew scripture, one year on the four Gospels, and one year on the twenty-three Epistles of the New Testament. He chooses the titles and texts for the following year's sermons each fall and gives them to Fred Elder so that hymns may be chosen to accompany the sermon effectively.

"It is a systematic way to cover all the significant books of the Bible every three years," he said. "It is true to Methodist history and I believe it is the most effective worship we can have."

Dr. Biggs believes that "Worship is the most important thing we do. Out of that grows missions, education, evangelism . . . sort of like building foot traffic in a department store. When the people fill the church and listen, they will give and they will join.

"When I served under Dr. Charles Allen in Houston, he told me, 'the secret is in knowing who will come to hear you.' Boston Avenue in Tulsa is a leader in mainline United Methodist religion. There are other churches in town serving specific niches, but I feel we continue to offer people an alternative. Liturgy with energy is what we offer. For the future, I feel we must continue to offer the people of the Tulsa area this alternative."

CHAPTER 19

A Milestone

B y the time Boston Avenue Church was one hundred years old, its membership had surpassed eight thousand with nearly three thousand enrolled in Sunday school and a staff of thirty.

An amazing number of programs had been developed within the church, each born to meet a need recognized by the pastor or one of the members. Today, members of the church of all ages serve on committees, commissions, and boards helping to plan the various programs and carry them out.

Boston Avenue's music program is extensive, with more than three hundred children, youth, and adults involved by 1993. Choirs include Kindergarten, First Grade, Jubilee (grades two and three), Altar (grades four and five), Chapel (middle school and high school), Festival Bell Ringers, and Chancel (adults).

Adult education opportunities include the School of Continuing Education and eighteen different Sunday school classes. Inquirers class (college age), New Directions (singles in their twenties and thirties), Finders (singles thirty and over), Young Disciples (couples in their twenties and thirties), Maranatha (couples in late twenties and thirties), Seekers (couples in thirties and forties), Pilgrimage (couples in late thirties through fifty), Heritage (persons in early forties through early fifties), Roundtable (persons in forties and fifties), Homebuilders (forties and above), New Covenant (persons forties through early sixties), Wesley Fellowship (couples and singles in their late fifties and above) Friendly (couples and singles in their sixties and older), Married Folks class (late sixties and above), Ephphatha (hearing-impaired persons), and Sunday Morning Bible Study, an informal Bible study group, and the Pastor's Bible Study group. Some of the newest classes are the Encouragers (an adult discussion group), Horizons (young adults in their mid-twenties desiring fellowship and spiritual growth), Singles with Children, and the New Life class.

The Bethel Bible Program began its congregational phase after completing its initial phase, and the Disciple Bible Study is another successful program in the church.

MORE
THAN A
BUILDING

189

Owl Camp, Vacation Bible School, summer music/drama workshops for grade schoolers, mission and choir tours, and camps for older children and youth. A Friends-In-Faith program and confirmation classes, which are held twice each year, prepare older children for the important step of becoming full and confirmed members of the church.

The School of Continuing Education has continued to grow and by 1993 there were nine hundred people involved in more than sixty classes twice each year.

Those with hearing impairments are served in several ways. The Ephphatha Sunday school class, Deaf Youth Fellowship, and Circle V all provide fellowship and activities. An interpreter provides signing for the hearing impaired during the church service every Sunday morning in a special section of the sanctuary.

The mission endowment fund had reached $122,000 by 1992, supporting a variety of programs. They include a strong and growing Volunteers in Missions (VIM) program which is sending medical teams to remote areas of the world. Area work teams, assistance with

A CENTURY OF MUSIC.
MAKING A JOYFUL SOUND HAS ALWAYS BEEN PART OF THE BOSTON AVENUE EXPERIENCE. THE CHILDREN'S CHOIR ON THE FACING PAGE SANG IN THE 1940S. BELOW, THE CHOIR AND CONGREGATION LIFT UP THEIR VOICES ON EASTER SUNDAY MORNING, 1991.

the Frances Willard Home, Neighbor for Neighbor, Cooperative
Ministries, and the Emergency Response program draw volunteers
from throughout the church on an
ongoing basis. Church members
may serve on such committees as
the commission on missions, the
family life committee, or the
Disciple Bible Study.

Outreach ministry
programs have been developed to
meet specific needs. The Respite
Care program offers opportunities
for parents with children who
have handicapping conditions to
have a "respite" or evening by
themselves. The Child Abuse
Prevention Service provides a
program for children in abusive or

MORE THAN A BUILDING

PEOPLE ARE THE HEART OF BOSTON AVENUE. CLOCKWISE FROM THE UPPER LEFT ARE CHURCH
MEMBERS CELEBRATING ADVENT IN BISHOPS HALL; CHILDREN PLAYING HOSPITAL IN A CHURCH
PROGRAM; DICK CLEVERDON AND HIS BOY SCOUTS; "FOREVER BEGINNING" PRODUCTION IN
1993; WOODY NAIFEH AT THE NITE OWL AND DAY CAMP AT THE NAIFEH RANCH; GORDON
SPENCER, A WONDERFUL TEACHER, WITH STUDENTS.

potentially abusive situations and nurturing classes for their parents. The Homebound Ministry program reaches members of the church who can no longer attend church services or activities. The Parents of Murdered Children group provides support for a very special group.

Throughout the church, volunteers serve in all these programs and in many other ways, from providing tours of the church to helping with office work. They drive for Meals on Wheels, help with the Sunday morning television broadcasts, drive the church vans for in-town and out-of-town trips, staff a clinic for low income families at Neighbor for Neighbor, and provide countless other services.

The building at Thirteenth and Boston, home to the church for sixty-five of its one hundred years, continued to evolve as members turned their attention toward the needs of the church in the twenty-first century. To celebrate the church's centennial, the family of long-time church member Mrs. W.K. Warren donated funds to commission two mosaics for the Great Hall. Adah Robinson's original plans had called for decorative murals on the north and south walls and recessed panels had been left for them, but the murals themselves were never completed due to the shortage of funds. In 1993, the church commissioned liturgical artist Angelo Gherardi of Park Ridge, Illinois, to design two mosaics representing the Old and New Testaments.

EFFECTS OF TIME
THE YEARS HAVE SOFTENED AND ENHANCED THE BLENDING OF THE ORIGINAL CHURCH BUILDING WITH THE EDUCATIONAL WING.

These were to be installed in Great Hall for the church's hundredth birthday in November, 1993.

Perhaps more than any other downtown building Boston Avenue Church is a Tulsa landmark, yet since 1957 Boston Avenue has been a one-way street north, so that motorists always have their backs to the church. By early 1993, plans had been made and many of the necessary approvals had taken place to change this. Plans call for both Main and Boston to become two-way streets between Tenth and Eighteenth. Being able to once again approach the magnificent and inspiring structure from the north, as was originally intended, will give a great joy to many.

Toward the Twenty-first Century

T he first century in the life of the Boston Avenue Church saw the building of a city and a church together—a "Twentieth Century church," as it came to be called when the modern cathedral was built at the corner of Thirteenth and Boston. And so it has been. Starting just before the start of the twentieth century in a little frontier town by people who had come to Indian Territory to build for themselves a future, this "worldly minded" congregation has never been content to keep things as they were in the past. Instead, through five generations, they have been busy shaping a better future for their church and their world.

Wise leaders have given the church their strength and dedication. Somehow, each pastor has seemed to be the right person for the church at the time, leaving his own mark, according to his interests and strengths. Families and individuals willing to give their prayers, presence, gifts, and service have constructed buildings which "impel them to worship." They have filled these buildings with inspirational preaching, music, art, learning, laughter, fellowhip, fun, caring ministries, and missions to take God's love out from the heart

DESCENDENTS OF THE PIONEERS
LEFT, JUDGE AND MRS. L. M. POE
AND THEIR FIVE SONS. ABOVE,
CAROLE GRAMMER,
GRANDDAUGHTER OF IDA BUCK
CONAWAY.

of the church sanctuary to people all over the world.

From the hard, struggling early years in which the Brewers, Conaways, Crutchfields, Wilsons, Clintons, Poes and others accomplished so much, each new generation has taken up the challenge. The Coles, Hunter Johnsons, Bradshaws, Clarks, Copples, Barnards, and Simpsons carried the church through the hard economic times of the depression. Then the Hollimans, Fields, Leonards, Bradleys, Bosts, Britts, Stuarts, Marshalls, Chapmans, Nelsons, Brannins, Nelsons, Johnsons, Enlows, Evanses, Browns, Loughridges, Warrens, Combses, Helmerichs, Monnets, Parrs, Coffeys, Farishes, Fosters, and hundreds of others have taken their place in the work that has made the church what it is.

As each generation has lived out its time and been "transferred above" (as was once said when a minister died) new generations have proved to be just as strong, dedicated, and resourceful as those before. Boston Avenue Church has grown and changed and adapted to the world around it and to the needs of its people, increasing the size of its building when the membership grew, accommodating those who did not let physical difficulties prevent them from joining in worshipping God in this church, reaching out into the community to

meet the needs there, and finding ways to serve those not able to be physically present to worship on Sunday morning.

Now, at the edge of a new century, the congregation pauses briefly to celebrate the achievements of the past. But what of the future? Will this "twentieth century church" now become a "twenty-first century church"?

Who will be the pastors and the caretakers in the future? No doubt, some will be the children, grandchildren, and great grandchildren of earlier members. Others will be new to the church and to Tulsa, probably coming from all over the world in this rapidly expanding global society.

Given their heritage, they will likely be "worldly" in the best sense of the word. They may be as dedicated and far seeing as those earlier members—builders constantly molding a church to meet the needs of their own time and to provide for future generations.

What programs will this church of the twenty-first century develop? What needs will it be called upon to meet? There may be a few glimpses, but God has given today's members no clearer vision of what this church will be in the year 2093 than the Reverend E.B. Chenoweth and his small band of worshippers had when they began in 1893. In the mud streets of this little frontier village they could not have envisioned one of Methodism's largest congregations meeting in a world-renowned cathedral, televising worship services weekly, jetting missionaries around the world, and using computers to keep in touch with some eight thousand members.

It does not matter that the future cannot be predicted. Tomorrow's God is today's God and yesterday's God. He will take Boston Avenue United Methodist Church where he wants it to go, through his people, just as he has done for the past one hundred years.

THE CLASS OF 1993
GRADUATING HIGH SCHOOL IN MAY, 1993 WERE
FRONT (L-R): MORGAN REICHMAN, JENNIFER BROWN, AMANDA DIXON, ANN HOUCHIN, DAVID WIGGS (MINSTER); MIDDLE (L-R): JOE CAROON, JOSH NEEL, JAY JANCO, RYAN SCHAFER; TOP (L-R): BRIAN MACIEL, JOSEPH WESTMORELAND, RUDD COFFEY, DAN BUNTING.

Jerry Zieglar and Eleanor Chenoweth

Early in 1993, Boston Avenue Church welcomed a very special visitor. Jerry Zieglar, the granddaughter of the Reverend Edgar Benson Chenoweth and Susan Eleanor Ervine Chenoweth, spent a few hours with several members of the church, sharing stories of her family. The daughter of the Chenoweth's daughter Eleanor Ruth, Jerry brought with her a tape of Mrs. Chenoweth (whom Jerry calls "Nanny" and her daughter Margaret reminiscing about the early days.

The tape, made when Mrs. Chenoweth was almost eighty-five, talks about her early life up until shortly after the Chenoweths left Tulsa. Susan Ervine and Edgar Chenoweth married July 15, 1891, and moved to Stewart, Colorado, where he was the circuit preacher. They then went to Denver where he took over the failing *Denver Dispatch* and *Rocky Mountain Methodist* and did some preaching. He invested his inheritance in trying to save the papers, but they collapsed when silver was demonetized.

After Denver, the Chenoweths moved to Cortez, Colorado, traveling by train. In Cortez, on the night Paul Duncan Chenoweth was born, Indians burned the church to the ground. "But the people in Cortez were wonderful people. They were always bringing us a things from their gardens, and I can remember them bringing us a washtub full of eggs. We didn't get but $300 or $400 per year but we managed to get along."

When they moved to Oklahoma, the Chenoweths and baby Paul traveled over the mountains in a spring wagon in what she called "a terrible trip."

When Margaret asked where the Reverend Chenoweth first preached in Tulsa, Mrs. Chenoweth chuckled and said, "In the saloons. Then we built a little shed and put benches in it and branches over the top—a brush arbor—and held services there in the summertime. By winter we had our church built. I was a charter member. There were seven charter members." Her voice was very proud and strong when she said, "That church is now Boston Avenue Church of Tulsa."

When Margaret asked if they had ever been back, Mrs. Chenoweth replied, "Oh, yes. We went back to visit and it was wonderful!"

Margaret Katherine Chenoweth was born in 1897, Eleanor Ruth in 1900, and Hattie Allien in 1902 or 1903.

Margaret had vivid memories of the time outlaws held up the family when she was three or four years old and Ruth was just a baby. "I remember that, too," Mrs. Chenoweth said. "We had gone to Brother Wilburn's to watch his sheepherders shear the sheep. It was nighttime before we started home and these outlaws stopped us. They thought Dad was the paymaster with the money to pay Brother Wilburn's sheepherders."

Margaret said, "That's the only time I ever remember Father being scared. He finally convinced them that he was not the man they wanted, and they let us go. Then they stopped us again and decided they wanted the wagon and the horses. He convinced them that he must take his family home. I'll never forget that he struck the horses to make them hurry away from there, which was totally unlike him. But the way he talked those men into letting us go is something I'll never forget."

"Yes," Mrs. Chenoweth said, "he really knew how to talk to people. He was so friendly, he made friends everywhere he went. People just seemed to want to do things for him."

Margaret commented that her mother had always seemed to be a very happy person, and asked her what advice she might give her grandchildren about how to make the most of life. "I think the secret is to make the most of what you have," Mrs. Chenoweth replied. "I've tried to do that and to enjoy everything I've done. Even when I had to ride in an airplane, I tried to enjoy it."

Carole Grammer

Carole Grammer is a third generation member of Boston Avenue Church. Her grandmother, Ida Buck Conaway, was one of the pioneer members, and her father, Loren A. Conaway, Jr., was baptized in the church in 1906 and was a member for many years.

Ida Conaway was one of the earliest Sunday school teachers in the brush arbor, teaching the young boys. One of her former students, Rex Evans, told Carole a few years ago, "She was so pretty. All the little boys were in love with her."

Carole calls herself an archivist and genealogist—not a historian—and has made a study of her family and the early years. She has fascinating stories to tell.

"There were a couple of very hard winters back to back in the mid-1880s, and so many of the cattle were killed there wasn't as great a need for ranch hands. It seemed like they either became outlaws or lawmen," she said.

Loren Conaway became a rather well-known law man, a Special Officer, and gained a lot of attention when he broke up a gambling game and arrested a dozen men. Strangely, when booked at the police station, all were named either "John Doe" or "Richard Roe." They were very prominent men, and were not happy about the zealous marshal who had arrested them.

"The city marshal relieved him of his duties," Carole said. "Not long after that, he was lured into an alley by someone who said they wanted to show him a pair of matched ponies, and was badly beaten by two men. He recognized them, and while he was recovering, contacted Bud Ledbetter, a famous lawman of the time in Muskogee. Ledbetter said they were walking the streets of Muskogee, bragging about what they had done. Conaway went to Muskogee, found them, and shot them dead. He said, 'They were gamblers and no good,'" she relates.

The newspapers reported that the clergymen of the town circulated a petition to have Officer Conaway reinstated after the gambling raid, and were successful. "He and Ledbetter pulled another raid not long after that and cleaned up the town. Judge Jennings was involved in that, too," Carole says.

She grew up in Tulsa, attending Burroughs, Pershing, Roosevelt and Central High. Because her mother, the former Elva Van Doeren, was Catholic, she grew up in that religion. Her father remained a Boston Avenue member.

In 1951, she married John Grammer, another Tulsa native, and they had one son, Randall Scott. She became a member of Boston Avenue Church several years ago and is active on the history and archives committee, even though she has moved to Arkansas.

She and John had frequently visited his parents in Siloam Springs, Arkansas, and John decided he wanted to move there. Carole says, laughing, "The marks from my heels dragging are still out there on Highway 412." But they moved to a lovely farm outside Siloam Springs, and she stays active in the Tulsa activities she enjoys, including the Tulsa Pioneers.

Patty Lee Poe

"Judge Poe was the wisest man I ever knew," Patty Lee says. "I loved my own father a great deal, but Judge Poe was a very special person."

Patty Lee was married for sixty-one years to Judge L.M. Poe's youngest son, Ned, who died in 1992. He had been ill for several years, but never lost his sense of humor. On their sixtieth anniversary, she went in and said, "Ned, do you know that we have been married sixty years today?" He looked up and grinned, and asked, "Both of us?"

"Judge and Mrs. Poe had nine children, but only six survived. The oldest, Myrtle Imogene, was an invalid all her life. But they took her to church and had a little metal chair they took her to movies in. Dr. Galloway used to visit her all the time."

"When Ned was growing up, he went to school at Horace Mann when it was an elementary school, and then to Lee when it was built. He graduated from Central High School in 1916.

"We married when I was nineteen and he was twenty-two. I worked on my master's degree while he finished law school. We were quite a curiosity on campus, because almost no one got married while they were in school at that time.

"Ned was born with a hole in his heart, but we didn't know it until the week after Pearl Harbor. The military wouldn't take him because of it. Heart trouble runs in the family."

Patty Lee is a small, slender, witty lady with a quick mind. A gifted poet, she has published a beautiful book of poetry called *Paper Trail*. She also grows prize winning flowers and is active in many organizations. She and Ned have one son, John, and a granddaughter, Suzanne Lee, who is twenty-three. They had a second son, Lewis, who died at the age of sixteen.

Elizabeth Wilson Smith

Elizabeth Ann Wilson was born when her father, Dr. Washington Milner Wilson, was sixty years old. "He and my mother, Elizabeth Baer, were married when he was fifty-eight and she was seventeen. His first wife, Susan Electra Davis, had died fifteen years before, when their daughter Julia was seven. Dr. Rice married my father and mother in the parsonage and they were married thirty-five years.

Elizabeth (the first daughter in the family was always named Elizabeth) remembers that the church was the center of Dr. Wilson's life. "Every Sunday afternoon we would go calling on different people, gathering pledges for the

church. He gave a lot of money to the Fifth and Boston church and the Thirteenth and Boston building. But he lost his money in the depression. He had owned the Wilson Apartments and lost them. We moved to Reservoir Hill and then to Fourteenth Place and Atlanta, which is now in the middle of the Broken Arrow Expressway.

"Norma Smallwood and her mother also lived in the Wilson Apartments, and that's where my parents lived when they were first married. Norma and my mother were friends. Norma was the first Miss America—1926—and married Thomas Gilcrease in 1928.

"I went to school at Barnard and Wilson, and then Will Rogers High School, which was new then. I sang in the choir for years and played in the gym at the church. We always sat in the fourth row in the middle pew in church.

"My father went on all the booster trips that the Tulsa businessmen took back east, and knew Will Rogers. He didn't think Will really was very good at rope tricks.

"When I was in high school, my father took a group of kids to the choir program at Westminster. We went to Coney Island and he rode the roller coaster and the rides with the kids. He was almost eighty at the time. I think my mother kept him young."

Ruth Clinton Kellam

"I remember that my Aunt Jane always wore white gloves and a flower of some kind," Ruth Clinton Kellam says. Aunt Jane is Jane Heard Clinton, wife of Dr. Fred Clinton.

Charles and Louise Clinton, Ruth's grandparents, had four children: Fred, Lee (Ruth's father), Paul, and Vera.

"Uncle Paul was younger and he was in real estate. He was a member of Boston Avenue. Aunt Vera married James H. McBirney, and they went to First Methodist. His father was a Methodist minister in Ireland. My mother's father was a Methodist minister in Tennessee." Ruth's mother was Susan

Merrill Clinton, and her brother was Walton Clinton.

"My brother Walton had a Creek allotment, but I didn't. I was born too late. I was born in 1907, and they had stopped the allotments in 1906." Their grandmother, Louise Clinton, was half Creek Indian.

"We had a sister, Celia Clinton, but she died when she was four of scarlet fever. They built a school on some of the family's land in west Tulsa and named it Celia Clinton. Now, it is on North Harvard."

"I remember the church at Fifth and Boston, particularly at Christmas time. They used to have a big Christmas tree and give oranges to all the children. They had a lot of church suppers in the basement."

Ruth married William Kone Kellam in 1931. He was a Presbyterian, but joined Boston Avenue in 1991.

Jean Hagler Pinkerton

"When J.R. Cole was the Sunday school superintendent, you didn't dare miss a Sunday; you might really miss something. He made it so much fun. He was always coming up with something new. And his wife was really nice," recalls Jean Hagler Pinkerton. "They lived in a big house in the 700 block of Boston, with a big porch around it."

Jean, the daughter of Joseph Don Hagler and Kate Teague Hagler, grew up in the church and married there.

Her father was one of the three men who built a toll bridge across the Arkansas River in 1904. "They moved that bridge later, and it still had the old iron sign on it that said 'They said we couldn't do it, but we did.' He was a banker from Missouri, and his father was a Methodist minister. He and my mother met and married in Arkansas, and they came to Tulsa the first time in 1898.

"We lived at Third and Boston, and that's

where my sister Margaret was born. My father died in 1909 when I was six. My mother was on the building committee for the Thirteenth and Boston building. I remember that Dr. Rice definitely didn't want a center aisle in the new building. 'I won't preach to an empty aisle,' he said."

Jean and James Carl Pinkerton were married by Dr. Grimes in the Rose Chapel in 1933. It's her favorite part of the church. "We were members of the Married Folks class. Alex Johnston was the teacher and he could really drum up the excitement. He built the class up until there were about a thousand in it. He was a flamboyant, exciting speaker." James Carl Pinkerton was a lawyer for the First National Bank and in private practice.

The Pinkertons had one son, James, born in 1936, who is a Tulsa lawyer like his father.

Eunice Mauzy

"Boston Avenue Methodist Church has always had the right minister at the right time. That's the Lord working," says Eunice Mauzy. She should know. A member for sixty-seven years, she's probably seen more history take place in the church than just about anyone else.

She came to Tulsa in 1925, having married Whit Mauzy in December of 1924. "At that time, I thought you should keep your membership in your home church for awhile, so I didn't move my membership for two years. I don't believe that now. I think you should change your membership whenever you move," she says.

Whit, a lawyer from the Shenandoah Valley in Virginia, had come to Tulsa after he graduated from the University of Virginia School of Law. Their home was near Swan Lake, then they later moved to 1532 South Gillette.

"The Married Folks Class was wonderful," she says. "It was organized in groups of twenty-five, and we looked after our own, doing what we could when people were sick or there were deaths or new babies. Alex Johnston is the one who built up the class. He was a wonderful teacher.

"During the depression, there wasn't much work for lawyers, and I sold underwear," the vivacious lady says. "Whit was very quiet, but very active in the church. He worked with the Boy Scouts and did a lot of things behind the scenes. His hobbies were his family, his church, the Boy Scouts and law—in that order. A bunch of lawyers got together to get him appointed U.S. Attorney, and he later was district judge. He died in 1970."

Eunice taught in the primary department of the Sunday School until Dr. Watts asked her to be Director of Children's Work. "I did that for nineteen years. Then I became a guide, showing people the church after Sunday morning worship service. I did that for another nineteen years," she says.

"The Rices were my favorites. I just adored them. I don't think anyone realizes how important the preacher's wives have been to this church. We went on a cruise for 'churchy people' while the Russells were at Boston Avenue. Dr. Russell had been asked to speak a few words at Galilee, but the guides sort of rushed us along. When we finally stopped, he spoke and Mary Jean, his wife, sang 'I Walked Today Where Jesus Walked.' I'll never forget it," she says.

The Mauzys had three children: Whit Junior, who graduated from MIT in engineering; Marcia, who lives in Edmond; and Eleanor, who lives in Salt Lake City. Eunice moved to a retirement home in Edmond a few years ago. More than a hundred people came to celebrate her ninetieth birthday in December of 1991.

She attends the New Covenant Methodist Church in Edmond with a friend and her son. "I'm in a Sunday School class with a lot of people the age of my grandchildren. They call me Foxy Grandma," she says with a twinkle in her eye.

People at Boston Avenue Church speak of her as "salty," "fiery," and "something else." "Foxy" fits right in.

Martha Jo Bradley

"My first memory of the church was going to a Christmas Eve service. There was a big tree in front of the pulpit, and all the children got gifts. I was five years old, and I especially remember that I had new shoes that buckled up the side," says Martha Jo Bradley.

The daughter of Mr. and Mrs. H.H. Copple, she was baptized by Dr. Barton and grew up in the church. She met John Bradley there when she came home from Stephens College and went to Epworth League where her parents were sponsors. He had come to Boston Avenue because when he moved to Tulsa, an aunt who had once dated Reverend Forney Hutchinson told him to look him up, that he had "a little church in Tulsa." Martha Jo remembers the church girls' basketball team in the twenties and thirties, coached by Velvine Stebbins. Mr. Landfair coached the boys' teams. "The church was the social hub during the depression years. There was always something going on."

She and John became Church Archivists in the mid-1980s, and devote many hours to making sure the church's history is preserved. "In 1941, the National Geographic ran a color picture of the church, and the article says 'Solomon's Temple was no more impressive than Boston Avenue Methodist Church.'"

She chuckles over the comments made by J.R. Cole, Jr., as head of the building committee for the Fifth and Boston church. He said the men were so proud of themselves and didn't want the women involved in the planning, so they ended up with both mahogany and oak in the sanctuary. That committee also planned a kitchen that was far too small for all the activities that went on there. "We still have the oak table from that building in the downstairs hall of the church," she says.

Kathryn Menard

Kathryn and Manly Carter were officers in the Married Folks Sunday School class at Boston Avenue before they even moved to Tulsa.

They had married in 1934 in Dallas, and a couple from their Sunday school class there, Red and Laura Upton, had moved to Tulsa. When the Carters moved here, they called the Uptons to ask about the best places to buy a house. "Before they even said 'hello,' they pointed their fingers at us and said, 'group leaders.'

"We probably would have moved back to Dallas at some point if it hadn't been for that class," Kathryn says. "Manly's fishing buddies all were in that class, and so many of our friends. At one time, the class had about twelve hundred members."

The Carters served as group leaders several times, edited the newsletter, and served the church in many other ways. The Carter children, Sue Ann and Mack, grew up in the church.

Manly and Kathryn were sponsors of the Young Adult class twice. Manly, angelic faced and slightly portly, was unforgettable when he dressed up as Aunt Jemima and hugged all the girls at the annual pancake breakfasts. Also unforgettable was the warm-hearted support always given by the Carters.

Kathryn continued to work in many ways in the church following Manly's death in 1968, serving as a choir mother for several years and working on the reception desk.

In 1973, Kathryn and the Reverend Ray Menard were married. He was an associate pastor at Boston Avenue for thirteen years, retiring three different times. In 1988, they moved to Methodist Manor.

Kathryn's favorite parts of the church building are the Rose Chapel and the tower, and her warmest memories are of the Married Folks class and the young adults she worked with.

WORKS CITED

BOOKLETS FROM THE ARCHIVES OF BOSTON AVENUE CHURCH

Boston Avenue Methodist Church, 50 Years.
Cole, Audrey. *A Twentieth Century Church.*
Crotchett, Anne. *Who's That in the Kitchen?*
Debo, Angie. *Jane Heard Clinton.*
Tulsa's Churches.

NEWSPAPERS

Our Brother in Red: The official publication of the Indian Mission Conference in Indian Territory and Oklahoma Territory.
The Tulsa Democrat.
The Tulsa Herald.
The Tulsa Tribune.
The Tulsa World.

BOOKS

Debo, Angie. *Tulsa, from Creek Town to Oil Capital.* Norman: University of Oklahoma Press, 1943.

Dunn, Nina Lane. *Tulsa's Magic Roots*. The Oklahoma Book Publishing Company, 1979.

Everly-Douze, Susan. *Tulsa Times, A Pictorial History.* 3 vol. Tulsa: World Publishing Company, 1986.

Gregory, Robert. *Oil in Oklahoma.* Tulsa: James C. Leake, 1976.

Tulsa 75. Tulsa: Metropolitan Chamber of Commerce, 1974.

Tulsa Spirit. Tulsa: Continental Heritage Press, 1979.

OTHER

Untitled script for a slide presentation on the history of Centenary United Methodist Church, Tulsa.